THE ISLES AND HIGH

Island Ho

The Isles
and **Highlands**
of
Western
Scotland,
Island Hopping
Bike Adventures

by Phil Horsley

An Essential Guide for the Touring Cyclist

CORDEE

ISBN 1 871890 83 7

British Library Cataloguing in Publication Data
A catalogue record for this book is available from the British
Library

All trade enquiries to :
CORDEE, 3a De Montfort Street, Leicester, LE1 7HD

Cover photographs by: David Paterson and Tim Hughes

This book is available from specialist equipment shops and
major booksellers. It can, along with a large selection of cycling
guides and maps, be obtained direct from the publishers.
Please write for a copy of our comprehensive stocklist of
outdoor recreation/sports, travel books and maps.

CONTENTS

THE HEBRIDES

THE NORTH-WEST HIGHLANDS

APPENDICES

MAP KEY

════	'A' Roads
═══	Other Roads
= = = =	Cycle Tracks
‑‑F‑‑	Ferry Crossings
S	Shop
▮	Pub/Hotel/Bar
☕	Café
i	Tourist Information Centre
▲	SYHA Hostel
△	Independent Hostel
⋏	Camp Site
⇌	Railway Station
✳	Place of Interest
+	Church
⊔	Castle
🚲	Cycle Hire and repair

The Western Highlands and Islands of Scotland

Cape Wrath
Tongue

North West Highlands

Lewis

Lochinver

Lairg

The Hebrides

Ullapool

Bonar Bridge

Harris

North Uist

Gairloch

Garve

Inverness

Benbecula

South Uist

Skye

Kyle of Lochalsh

Loch Ness

Barra

Mallaig

Ardnamurchan

Fort William

Roads to the Isles

Mull

Oban

Iona

Loch Awe

Inveraray

Jura

Strathclyde

Glasgow

Islay

Ardrossan

Kintyre

Arran

INTRODUCTION

It was one of those perfect evenings. The sun, a couple of hours from setting the sky aflame, turned the sea to silver, with the islands shimmering offshore. We had followed our evening meal with pints of Guinness in the company of a couple of Wallace – lookalikes and the New Zealand barmaid, and were looking for a spot to camp. We floated along the lochside road in utter tranquility with not a vehicle in hearing. A seal, poking its head from the loch, watched us pass by, as did the herd of red deer on the mountainside. Yet the morning had begun with a thick, clinging mist, and a ferry bobbing and weaving like a fairground duck. Such are the contrasts of a cycle journey through the Western Highlands and Islands of Scotland.

There are words to describe the scenery, but when you're in its midst, it just takes your breath away. At the same time there is something very sad about the reminders of a culture thriving until not so very long ago. Why do so few people live up here? The answer is, they used to, but were either 'cleared' to make way for sheep and deer, or were driven out by the harsh realities of the climate. Stornoway, after all, lies further to the north than both Moscow and Labrador in Newfoundland. For the cyclist from the town or city, the shock of cycling in this most dramatic corner of Britain is exhilarating and awe-inspiring. You cannot be prepared for the experience, but you must be prepared for the distances, and the weather. Whether you are intent upon a long weekend or a month or two's travel, this guide is for you.

For the purposes of this guide, the region is divided into four, each with one or more 'loops'. To the south, the cycle-runs in *Strathclyde* are literally on Glasgow's doorstep, and, through Oban, provide a gateway to the north. The *Roads to the Isles* section offers a complete contrast with an exhilarating coastal run, and a route through the highest mountains in Britain. To the west of Lochalsh are the *Hebrides*, Skye and the Outer Isles, places so unlike anywhere else in Britain. The *North-West Highlands* lead to the most remote corner of the British mainland and the 600 feet high cliffs at Cape Wrath. The White-Tailed Sea Eagle, a larger cousin of the Golden Eagle, has been reintroduced to the Western Highlands and Islands after an absence of seventy years. Isn't it time to discover the place for yourself?

TRAVEL FROM WITHOUT, AND WITHIN

Rail
From the mainline railway stations in Glasgow and Edinburgh, two lines carry trains to the northwest; the West Highland line to Oban and Fort William/Mallaig from Glasgow Queen Street; and the line to Perth and Inverness with connections to Kyle of Lochalsh and Wick/Thurso. Mostly these trains are two and three car 'Sprinters' with limited capacity for carrying cycles. Advance booking is recommended, and a fee payable (£3 per trip in 1996). The situation may be affected by rail privatization.

Air
There are international airports at Glasgow, Edinburgh and Inverness, with smaller airstrips on Islay, Skye, Barra, Benbecula, Lewis (Stornoway) and at Wick. The majority of internal flights are operated by British Airways Express (Loganair).

Ferries
Most of the island ferries are operated by Caledonian Mac-Brayne Ltd (Calmac), a publically owned company, though a few of the smaller ferries are privately run. Details of the relevant ferries are given in the Appendices. It is always a good idea to check for cancellations, delays etc., the sea being what it is, but it usually takes exceptionally bad weather to affect the running of the ferries.

Other Possibilities
If you are stuck, do not despair, for there are other possibilities. Most places are served by buses, and whereas these are most often postbuses or minibuses, the driver will help you if he can. The transporting of other peoples goods and chattels may not be condoned, but it has long been the practice.

Local drivers will often help you out, too, especially on the Outer Isles, where pickups can be seen in significant numbers.

CYCLE SHOPS AND CYCLE HIRE

Cycle shops are noted in the text where appropriate. Cycle Hire establishments may not be able to help with a problem with your bike, but they just might. Please note that cycle shops are a good distance apart, often a day or two's cycling. It is a good idea to carry enough equipment to ensure that you can at least give your bike First Aid if required.

ACCOMMODATION

Hotels/Bed and Breakfast Accomodation

There is a plentiful supply of such accomodation on the mainland, less so on the Islands. Lists can be obtained from the Tourist Boards, and Tourist Information Centres (TIC's) are particularly helpful, many operating a 'Book-A-Bed-Ahead' system. TIC's are listed in the text and the Appendices.

Hostels

The Scottish Youth Hostel Association (SYHA) manage a fine variety of hostels throughout the area. Membership is required, either contact Head Office, or join at the first hostel. In addition, the Western Highlands and Islands are well provided with independent hostels, which vary in size and quality, and cost between £3 and £9 a night. On the Outer Hebrides the Gatliff Trust hostels are small, locally run, and operate with the help of the SYHA. Some are in restored, thatched, 'blackhouses'.

Camping

There are a few campsites, usually operated in conjunction with barracks of caravans. In the larger towns, Oban, Inverness and Ullapool, you will be enthusiastically directed towards them. Elsewhere 'wild' camping is not discouraged, except on farm-land and 'unfriendly' estates. In practice much of the land is too wet to camp on with any degree of comfort, and it invariably pays to consult the locals who will often point you in a helpful direction.

HAZARDS

Traffic

Lots of Highland roads are relatively traffic-free and an absolute joy on which to cycle. Some are not, notably the A9, A82, A83 and A85, though everything is comparative, and the traffic on these roads is but a mere trickle against the clogged arteries of England. The English do not possess, in contrast, 'single track roads with passing places'. On these a cyclist can usually proceed sedately and allow traffic to 'do it's own thing', but the author has been knocked off his bike on these roads, essentially because he was riding too near the road edge. So, maintain your own road space, and if this means 'working' the passing places, then this is infinitely preferable to a brush with the verge.

On the major roads in the country, if there is a pavement, do not hesitate. Use it to cycle on. It may be illegal but one day this will be officially accepted and cycle paths provided.

There is a further traffic hazard in the Western Highlands. Many of the road junctions have reminders to drive on the left, and one farmer at least has put up a notice 'Achtung – Sheep' (presumably he assumed that 'Sheep' is a Euro-Word and the English is 'hogget' or 'tup'). The serious side to the huge influx of foreigners to Scotland is the increasing number of accidents caused. Beware, as a cyclist, you are vulnerable.

The Midge

Para Handy, of the good ship 'Vital Spark', told of the Dervaig midges, how the elders sent the youngsters into the tents of campers to test the blood groups to ensure a good quality night's feasting. The midge does not live on blood, it is simply that the female requires the stuff to ripen her eggs, and unfortunate for us that her hormones operate this way. There are lots of deterrents; a force 10 gale, mosquito netting, a good peat fire and no chimney, a plug of condor triple strength and a good briar pipe designed to operate like a blast furnace, and strong chemicals, fortunately contained in tubes or bottles. In extreme circumstances, when the midges are thick enough to blot out the sun, these may be sufficient simply to hold the midge in orbit at a distance of one inch from the head. The simple answer is to stay on the bike until the next sou'Wester comes ripping in from the Atlantic.

The Climate

Generally, over a year, there are more wet days in the Western Highlands than dry ones. Do not let this put you off, for any Highlander will tell you of those glorious spells of unbroken sunshine and no wind, when there is no better place to be than where you are, often in May and September (or another month if you happen to be there in May or September). It is, however, best to be prepared, should the glorious spell break down temporarily.

Perhaps a mention should be given to raingear. There are still cyclists to be found who prefer the old-fashioned cape and sou'Wester. The sou'Wester is brilliant. A better hat for a squall has yet to be invented, and what is more, they are rarely obtainable only in day-glo colours. Unfortunately the cape has disadvantages, for, in a wind, not only does it take on some of the characteristics of a barrage balloon, but it is also highly susceptible to horizontal rain. On balance it is better to go either for sleek, modern raingear of a composite fabric which keeps you dry when being sprayed with a water cannon, and allows the breeze to lightly skip away into one's slipstream, or full tartan drapes, plus fours and deerstalker.

If the worst comes to the worst and you find yourself holed up in a bothy for three days with only Kenneth McKellar, a can of Irn Bru and a MacBraynes timetable for company, you can always pass the hours working out who you would rather be with, and with what, or, alternatively, pick eight records.

CYCLING

Cycling in the Western Highlands and Islands is one of life's great pleasures. You will meet other cyclists, Scots, English, European, American, all drawn to this breathtaking quarter of Scotland. Do not expect the cycling to be easy, but there will always be compensations; the freewheeling descent following the climb; a mindblowing sunset at the end of a grim day; the hotel bar rocking with laughter as you escape the rain.

Be Prepared

Fuel the engine. Always carry a nibble, preferably something that will keep you going for a few hours if you get caught out in the middle of nowhere, miles from the nearest deep-fried, battered, Mars bar.

Care for the machine. The three most common mechanical problems are punctures, worn brakes and broken spokes. Avoid punctures by using high-pressure tyres inflated hard, but road-side repairs are easier if you carry a spare tube as well as the tyre levers and a puncture repair kit. Keep an eye on the brakes and regularly adjust appropriately. The big descents are apt to burn up the rubber. Carrying a load increases the threat of broken spokes. Even if you do not know how to replace one, or are reluctant to carry a freewheel remover and workshop vice, it is a good idea to carry a spoke key, using it to adjust the other spokes to get you to the nearest bike shop, and a couple of spare spokes of the correct size (taped to your frame) for them to use if they are out of your size. For the mechanically minded, four-crossing the spokes on the freewheel side of the rear wheel does work, but be sure to bring along a spare extra-long spoke or two just in case. Your tool kit should also include allen keys and spanners to fit your bike, a spare bowden cable to replace a broken gear or brake cable, and a lubricant (WD40, GT85 or equivalent) for regular use on chain, cogs and bearings. Be prepared if you intend to cross the sea in a small boat with your bike lashed to the rail. Salt water can be very corrosive. Which brings me back to the 'engine' and the unfortunate influence an unruly sea crossing can have on it. The author is not one of the world's natural sailors, and admits to having felt queasy on the Leeds and Liverpool canal. However, since discovering the wrist bands with the pressure point on the pulse, he is a changed man, and would quite happily bob around the Minch in a pea-green boat.

The Routes in this Book

The routes in this book have been arranged in loops, so that, whatever time you have available, be it a few days or a couple of months, you can add together the mileage of the stages, and work out an appropriate loop. Bear in mind, if timing is all important, and you wish to cycle on the Islands, that a careful reading of the ferry timetable is required.

Recommended Maps
This guide is designed to provide all the information you may require, but many cyclists will feel the need to carry a road map, and there is none better than the Ordnance Survey 'Travelmaster' series, at a scale of 1:250,000 (1 inch to 4 miles).

Author's Personal Note
I was asked the other day, which, of all the routes in this book, is the best. Of course, it is an impossible question, but my personal favourite would be an island run; Arran, across Kintyre to Islay and Jura, timed to catch the weekly ferry to Oban, Mull, Ardnamurchan to Mallaig, ferry to Barra and up through the Outer Hebrides. It is not simply that these are 'other worlds', so different from anywhere else in Britain, but also the combination of ferry crossings and cycling is a brilliant way to travel and the constant presence of the sea adds an extra dimension.

Should I be offered just one run, of one or two days duration, to wrap up, take home and have available to do every week or so, it would be the coastal run from Drumrunie Old Lodge, north of Ullapool, through Lochinver and Drumbeg to Kylesku. The constantly changing patterns of sea and mountains, the colours and textures are truly exceptional.

TIMESCALE

c. 6000 BC to c.1500 BC	As the Ice Age receded Scotland gradually became settled. The earliest hunters and fishers took to farming and by 2000 BC were sufficiently developed to construct the standing stones at Callanish. The Western Highlands and Islands are littered with remnants of this period; circles, standing stones, burial grounds etc.

c.1500 BC to 450 AD	During the Bronze and Iron Ages, Scotland was inhabited by various tribes, speaking a Celtic language. In the north these people were known as Picts, and, later, they conducted a running battle with the Romans.	*In England* 55 BC Caesar lands in Kent. 121 AD Hadrians wall constructed.
450 AD to 750 AD	A Gaelic-speaking tribe from Ireland, the Scots, founded a kingdom called Dalriada, based in Argyll. With the help of St Columba, using fair means or foul, they became the dominant force in Scotland.	547 AD the Angles began to settle eastern England.
750 AD to 1263	From the late 8c the Vikings began their raids in the north. In 839 a gaelic chief, Kenneth MacAlpin, became King of a united Scotland, but the Viking incursions continued, and by the 11c the power of Earl Thorfinn the Mighty embraced most of western Scotland as well as the north and north-east. They were eventually defeated by King Alexander the Second at the battle of Largs in 1263.	878 AD King Alfred, in England, burnt the cakes preparing to fight the Danes. 1066 Battle of Hastings.
1263 to 1692	The Islands and Western Highlands were held by clan chiefs 'on behalf of' the monarch, though the Lords of the Isles, a grouping of clans held together by the MacDonalds, assumed an attitude of self-determination until subdued by King James the Fourth in 1493. The rest of Scotland at this time was fighting for its life against the English.	1220 The construction of Salisbury Cathedral was begun. 1296 King Edward the First of England invades Scotland. 1530's the Reformation. 1587 Mary Queen of Scots beheaded. 1642-1649 English Civil War.

| 1692 to 1745 | The deep religious and political divisions within 17c English society had their effect on the Highlands. In 1692 the Highland clans were forced to take an oath of loyalty to the new King, William of Orange, and when the MacDonalds of Glencoe were slow to acquiesce, they were massacred by the soldiers under Campbell leadership.
Four times in the next forty years the Jacobites tried to restore the Stuarts to the throne, ending in a devastating defeat at Culloden in 1745, with 1200 Highlanders slaughtered in less than an hour. | 1707 The Act of Union between England and Scotland.
1742 Handel writes 'the Messiah'. |
| 1745 to 1886 | The Government made the Highlanders pay dearly. The region was garrisoned, the clan structure disbanded, gaelic suppressed and even the wearing of the kilt and the playing of the bagpipes proscribed.
The changes introduced a new breed of absentee landlord bent on exacting an income from the Highland estates to support their metropolitan lifestyle. Over a hundred year period more than half a million people were forced off the land to make way for sheep farming and, then, deer estates. Many emigrated to the colonies, others filled the Glasgow slums or joined the newly formed Highland regiments. Sickness and shipwrecks took a heavy toll. | 1825 Opening of the Stockton to Darlington Railway.
1815 Battle of Waterloo. |

1886 to the Present Day   The Crofting Act of 1886 stabilised the Highland communities, and public finance has brought some of the Twentieth Century's wealth to the Highlands and

Islands, but depopulation continues and job opportunities are few. Secondary schooling often involves the pupils lodging away from home, and Tertiary education means leaving the area. The expectation is that over 75% of school-leavers must migrate through lack of jobs. It is ironic that the remoteness, lack of development and sterility of landscape are becoming an attraction for the expanding tourist industry.

SOME MEN OF SIGNIFICANCE

H.T. Munro, mountaineer, listed all the mountains in Scotland over 3000' high, separated from another by a dip of 500' or more. There are 276 and they are known as 'Munros'.

The MacCrimmons were hereditary pipers to the MacLeods of Dunvegan, and the greatest piping family of all time. Their 17c and 18c compositions, the pibrochs (piobaireachd), form the core of the classical music of the bagpipes, in contrast to the whimsical reels, strathspeys, marches and jigs.

Rob Roy MacGregor, full-time bandit, was a member of the MacGregor clan outlawed for continued misdemeanor, often bloody.

General Wade built military roads in Scotland to subdue the Clansmen after the 1715 uprising.

Prince Charles Edward Stuart, the Young Pretender, was 25 when he landed near Arisaig. (see separate section)

The Duke of Cumberland ('Butcher' to his enemies) faced the Highland army at Culloden. He was four months younger than Bonnie Prince Charlie.

Thomas Telford (1757 to 1834), the orphan son of a Dumfries shepherd, built roads, bridges and piers all over Scotland, many of which are still in use.

John Loudon Macadam, born in Ayrshire, (originally a MacGregor but the family changed the name when the clan was outlawed), had his system of road building officially accepted in 1817.

ECOLOGICAL DECLINE

The Western Highlands and Islands today are less a natural wilderness than a degraded, eroded near-desert, with the surviving wildlife merely remnants of a fabulous natural abundance on land, sea and air. Today there is relatively little food grown in the area, for people or winter feed for animals, comparatively little power generated and very little timber grown as a fuel or building material.

The soil is naturally thin. The Western Highlands are the wettest part of Europe, and rainfall exceeds potential evaporation throughout the year, restricting the maturation of plants and regeneration. The soil does not naturally build up. For centuries it was farmed as a renewable resource, primarily by cattle, which fertilized as they grazed, and by the regenerating woodland. Overgrazing by sheep in the last 250 years has had a disastrous effect on the quality of the soil, and only small pockets remain of the natural woodland. The once extensive system of hill field drains have blocked up through lack of care, further degrading the soil.

The sheep is responsible for the prevention of woodland regeneration, without which the soil continues to deteriorate, leading to poorer grazing for the sheep. This, and the lack of cover in winter, has resulted in high losses at lambing time, up to 50%. Sheep farming in the Highlands is hugely subsidized by the E.C., and without the grants would not be profitable today. A couple of centuries ago hill farmers and crofters grew barley, oats and potatoes enough to feed themselves. This fertility has been eroded over the years.

Although large areas of the Highlands are maintained for the sport of hunting red deer, grouse shooting and fishing, the quality of all three has diminished. The quarter of a million red deer in the Highlands pose a huge threat to anyone wanting to grow anything, as the large garden fences testify, yet deer malnutrition is a serious problem. For complex reasons there has been a steep decline in grouse 'bags' in the last 50 years. Wild salmon are threatened in many ways by salmon farming, disease transmission, chemical pollution and genetic drift among them. In the sea the overfishing of mackerel and shellfish threatens to lead to a similar collapse which saw the disappearance of herring.

Today, huge estates regularly change hands for millions of pounds. Half of Scotland is in the hands of 579 landowners, and about two thirds of the landowners in the Highlands are absentees. The feudal land ownership pattern may not have been the sole cause of the social and ecological decline in the Highlands and Islands, but the estate owners have overseen its occurence. The example of estate owners receiving government subsidy for *not* carrying out a threat to plant with conifers areas which are ecologically worthy of conservation, typifies their approach to the region.

The largest single landowner is the Forestry Commission, which, with its blanket planting of the imported species, Sitka Spruce and Lodgepole Pine, has done more than most to encourage environmental and ecologial deterioration.

The 'Highland Problem' as defined by Fraser Darling after the last war remains largely the same fifty years later.

Strathclyde

STRATHCLYDE

The 'Highlands' of Scotland south of Glasgow? Surely this cannot be true? Arran and Kintyre have traditionally been part of the Highlands, and, though mellowed somewhat by the proximity of the 'Weegies', they undoubtedly belong more to the Highlands than to motley southern Scotland.

All three routes detailed in this book begin with a ferry crossing. For the embarkation of a cycle journey to the Western Highlands and Islands this is an entirely appropriate genesis. Yet, it also throws up a couple of problems, for the ferry from the north end of Arran to Kintyre is seasonal, operating from April to October, and the ferry from Port Askaig to Oban only sails on a Wednesday (1996). So, whether you are choosing one of these routes as part of a long journey further north, or taking a long weekend run from Glasgow, you may have to plan your route with care.

ARRAN (ARAINN)

Brodick – Machrie – Lochranza	**21.5 miles**
Brodick – Sannox – Lochranza	**13 miles**

Ferries. Arran is served by Calmac ferries from Ardrossan to Brodick (approx 6 a day), and a smaller ferry to Claonaig on Kintyre from Lochranza (approx 10 a day, but this is a seasonal service operating from early April to mid-October). A combined ticket in 1996 cost around £6, including the bicycle.

Arran is mild enough to grow palms, fuschias, acacias etc, and moist enough for Lochranza to get a mention in the Guinness Book of Records as having the most days in a year without sunshine. Its situation, in the middle of the Clyde estuary places it uniquely between the mainland and the Highlands. Arran is primarily a tourist resort, and within a hop, skip and jump of Glasgow, yet historically has been part of the Highlands, sharing many of the features, and specifically part of the Viking empire of Scottish islands. Like the other Hebridean islands most people live on the coastal belt, and numbers are declining, from, in 1801 a Gaelic speaking population of 5,179, to less than 3,500 mainly English speaking souls today.

Pre 1766 most people lived in 'clachans', little farm villages consisting of 'black houses', of stone and thatch, home to man and beast alike, with a communal, patriarchal way of life based on the clan system. In that year John Burrel was asked by the Duke of Hamilton to devise better ways of exploiting the island. By 1829 whole tracts of the north were given over to sheep and the island ruled by a factor, evicting where he chose, on behalf of a remote landlord, with farmers now fighting each other for the better tenancies. Most of the enterprises set up to provide employment failed, and, for many, emigration was the only answer, until tourism arrived.

The Dukes of Hamilton, Arran's owners, in the 19c blocked every attempt to make the island a holiday resort, and only after 1895 were ducal restrictions lifted and villas, shops and boarding houses began to spring up. Nevertheless, from 1868 steamer services brought more and more visitors. In 1890 The Caledonian Railway Co set out to wrest the Ardrossan – Brodick trade from their hated rivals, the Glasgow and South Western Railway.

15

Arran

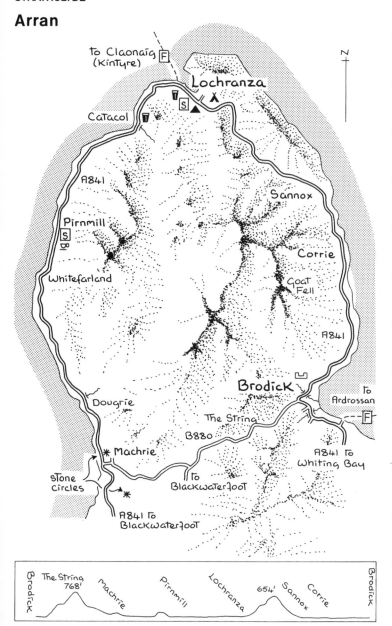

'Glasgow to Arran in 90 minutes' they advertised. This led to a speed war with the magnificent paddle steamers 'Duchess of Hamilton'(C.R.) and 'Glen Sannox'(GSWR) racing each other, with occasional collisions, across the Firth. This continued until 1908, and in 1923 both companies became part of the L.M.S.

For the cyclist on Arran, there are alternative routes from Brodick to Lochranza. The first takes 'The String' a trans-island climb to 768 feet engineered in 1817 by Thomas Telford, followed by the fabulous coastal run up the western shore, with its white beaches and panorama of Kintyre. The second takes the eastern shore, around Goat Fell, then the rather exciting Boguillie Pass,up to 654 feet and the long, lonely descent to Lochranza.

Brodick ☕ 🍴 🅂 ⓘ The present village was moved here in the 19c by the Eleventh Duke of Hamilton, to be a more 'suitable' distance from the castle. The castle, their ancestral home, was well battered over the years, and completely restored in 1844. The Isle of Arran Folk Museum is at Rosaburn.

Machrie Moor has the Tormore group of monoliths and cairns, including eight stone circles.

Catacol The village was built by the Eleventh Duke to house people cleared off their crofts to make way for sheep and deer.

Lochranza ☕ 🍴 ⓘ The castle ruins are picturesque, 16c, on the site of an earlier one. In 1847 this was the island's main fishing port for herring, but by 1905 the herring had gone, overfished out of existence.

Goat Fell, 'Gaoith Bheinn' (the Hill of the Winds), at 2866 feet, is Arran's highest mountain.

Corrie 🅂 🍴 High Corrie was the birthplace of Daniel Macmillan, founder of the publishing house, and grandfather of Harold. Just north of the village, on open hillside, white posts marked the 'measured mile', for Clyde-built ships on trial.

Sannox Traces of limekilns remain, as do the quarries from which barytes was extracted.

▲   Lochranza tel. (01770) 830631
△   Corrie Croft, North High Corrie, tel. (01770) 302203
🚲   Brodick Cycles tel. (01770) 302460

Kintyre and Knapdale

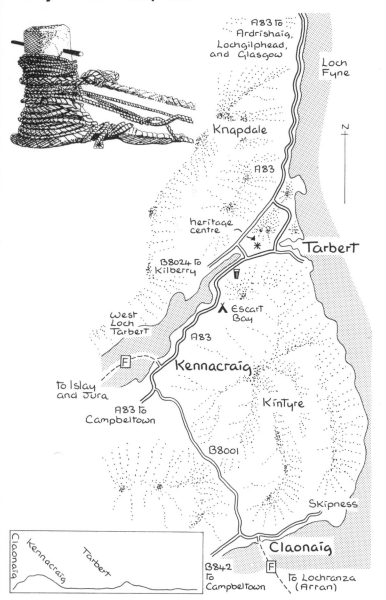

A83 to
Ardrishaig,
Lochgilphead,
and Glasgow

Loch
Fyne

Knapdale

A83

N

heritage
centre

Tarbert

B8024 to
Kilberry

West
Loch
Tarbert

Escart
Bay

A83

F

Kennacraig

to Islay
and Jura

Kintyre

A83 to
Campbeltown

B8001

Skipness

Claonaig   Kennacraig   Tarbert

Claonaig

B842
to
Campbeltown

F

to Lochranza
(Arran)

18

KINTYRE and KNAPDALE

Claonaig – Ardrishaig   **21.5 miles**

Kintyre is famous, firstly for the Paul McCartney dirge recorded with Tom Wilson, Pipe Major of the Campbeltown Pipe Band, and secondly for being the angle of the dangle above which male attachments are not officially allowed to be seen.

From Claonaig the open road crosses Kintyre, and it's a bit of a shock meeting the A83. Lorry traffic will probably increase as a new ferry is due to open from Campbeltown to Ulster.

Skipness S The castle is a typical 13c West Highland pile held by the Lords of the Isles, then the Campbells, for the King. Nearby Kilbrannan Chapel is late 13c, on the foundations of an older one, dedicated to St Brandon.

Kennacraig The ferry terminal to Port Ellen and Port Askaig on Islay. (see appendices)

Tarbert S 🍴 ☕ ⓘ The centre of the Loch Fyne herring industry in the 18/19c, with all the ancillary trades, net-making, chandlery, kippering etc. Now the harbour has yachts.

The very ruinous castle was probably built in 1325 by Robert the Bruce, Tarbert occupying a stategic position.

When Magnus Barefoot, King of Norway, launched an invasion in 1098, the Scots King Edgar, already occupied on the English frontier, decided to keep the Norsemen at bay by agreeing they could take any island around which they could travel. Magnus wanted Kintyre, so he sat at the tiller of his longboat as it was dragged across the isthmus. 'Tarbert' means 'isthmus'. The town has a new heritage centre.

🚲   (cycle hire) Sailmakers, Garval Rd, Tarbert (01880) 820287

Crinan and Kilmartin

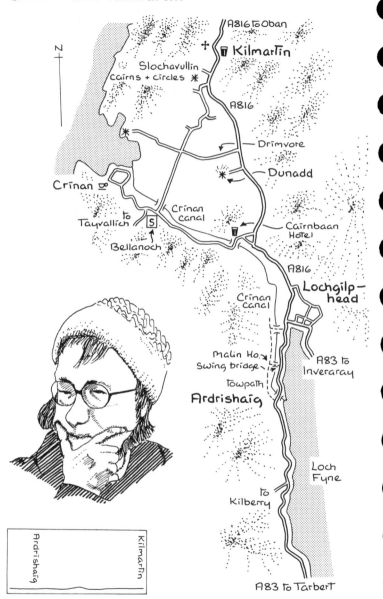

A816 to Oban

✝ 🍺 Kilmartin

Slochavullin
Cairns + circles ✳

N

A816

Drimvore

✳ — Dunadd

Crinan ⚓

Crinan
canal

to
Tayvallich ⑤

Bellanoch

🍺 ← Cairnbaan
Hotel

A816

Lochgilp-
head

Crinan
canal

Malin Ho.
Swing bridge

A83 to
Inveraray

Towpath

Ardrishaig

Loch
Fyne

to
Kilberry

A83 to Tarbert

Ardrishaig	Kilmartin

CRINAN and KILMARTIN

Ardrishaig – Kilmelford   **25miles**

Unfortunately the 'main road' cycling on the A83 and the A816, even with breaks at Ardrishaig and Crinan, makes it difficult to appreciate the true nature of this cradle of Scotland. The area feels transitory, with its constantly changing moods and textures.

Ardrishaig 🍴 Ⓢ The village was built around the pier and southern entrance to the Crinan Canal. The 9 mile canal saves a 130 mile sea voyage. Designed by John Rennie, and opened in 1801, it had to be virtually rebuilt 16 years later by Thos. Telford. The herring boats have largely been replaced by yachts.

Lochgilphead 🍴 Ⓢ ☕ ⓘ No longer a herring port or market town, but a tourist centre and the administrative centre of Argyll.

Dunadd The rock rears out of the plain of Moine Mhor (the Great Moss). The fort on the summit was the centre of Dalriada; the place where the first 'Scots', King Fergus and his brothers, came from Ireland in the 5c, and from which, by fair means and foul, they established their authority over the Picts until, in 863 , Kenneth MacAlpin was able to be crowned the first King of Scotland. It is claimed that the Stone of Destiny was first used here, though it was certainly different from the Stone of Scone taken by Edward the First, and returned to the Scots in 1996.
The surrounding area is rich in antiquities, standing stones, circles, crosses, cairns etc.

Kilmartin 🍴 The churchyard has a wonderful assembly of early medieval slabs and memorials.

Carnasserie The late 16c tower house was the home of John Carswell, first Protestant Bishop of the Isles and writer of the first book to be printed in Gaelic. He was remembered mainly for the day of his funeral, for the weather was so bad his body could not be ferried across to the burial ground. Thereafter the worst that could be said of any day was that it was nearly as bad as the day of Carswell's funeral.

Ardfern At the end of the peninsula is the whitewashed

21

Craignish castle. The tip of the peninsula overlooks the Gulf of Corrievreckan, and the noise of the whirlpool and the tide-race can often be heard.

 Crinan Cycles, Ardrishaig. (01546) 603511

The Abbey of St Mary, Iona. Photo. David Paterson

23

Loch Melfort and Loch Feochan

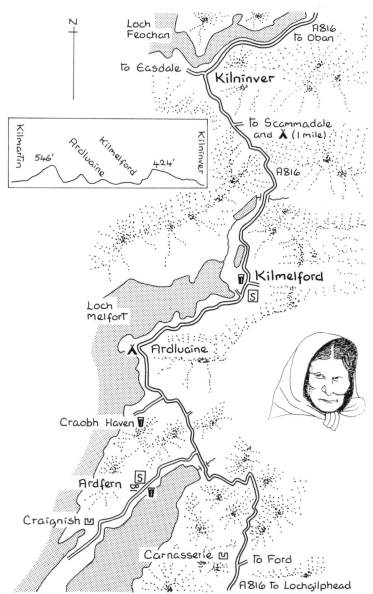

Loch Feochan

A816
To Oban

To Easdale

Kilninver

To Scammadale
and ✗ (1 mile)

A816

Kilmartin · 546' · Ardluaine · Kilmelford · 424' · Kilninver

Kilmelford

Loch Melfort

Ardluaine

Craobh Haven

Ardfern

Craignish

Carnasserie

To Ford

A816 To Lochgilphead

LOCH MELFORT and LOCH FEOCHAN

Kilmelford – Oban   **14 miles**

The A816 ducks and dives between sea inlets and the intervening hills. It is not spectacular, nor is it particulary pleasant cycling, but it is refreshing and there are wonderful westward vista's of the ocean with islands bobbing about like dumplings in a stew.

Arduaine The gardens have one of the finest collections of rhodedendrons in Scotland, spectacular in the spring.

Glen Euchar (Scammadale) Green mounds mark the Sabhal nan Cnamham (Barn of Bones), where Alexander Colkitto Macdonald is said to have collected all the Campbells from the glen into a barn, and burned them alive.

Kilninver Traditionally the coffins of the illustrious dead were shipped out from Carraig nan Marbh at Kilninver to Mull, and on to Iona.

Around Oban various roads can be used to avoid the traffic thoroughfares.

Loch Nell At its foot is the 300' long Serpent mound, claimed to be the most perfectly formed such prehistoric relic in Europe, dedicated to Ophiolatry, the worship of snakes.

Oban and Loch Etive

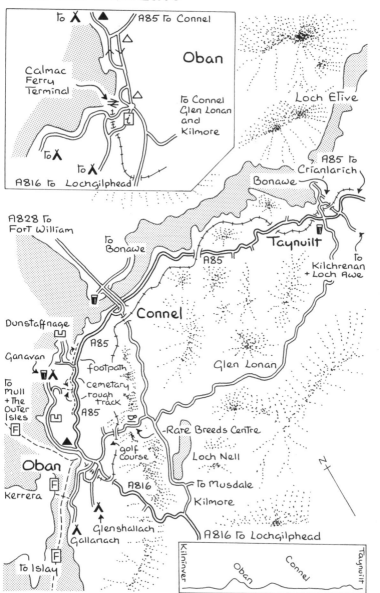

OBAN and LOCH ETIVE

Oban – Taynuilt   **11.5 miles**

Oban is the Mecca of the Western Highlands. Sooner or later you will pass through it, and hang about in one of the cafes watching the nationalities mingle.

Departing by train. Oban is the end of the line to Glasgow. The trains, on average two a day, are 'Sprinters', with limited, but bookable, accomodation for bicycles. Advance booking is strongly advised.

Departing by ferry. The main ferry is over to Mull, but other ferries depart for Lismore and Barra and South Uist. Cyclists don't need to book, simply buy a ticket in advance and turn up with your bike at the car deck entrance.

Departing by road. The main roads around Oban are busy, particularly the A85 north to Connel, a narrow, twisting road. Either make illegal use of the pavement as far as Dunbeg, or take to the minor roads inland, though the climb over to the Rare Breeds Centre is not without punch.

Staying in Oban. There are lots of B & B's, a SYHA hostel and two independent hostels. Fly-camping is heavily discouraged, but there are 3 camp sites, all about 2 miles out of town, at Gallanach and Glenshallach to the south, and Ganavan to the north.

Oban 🍴 ⑤ ☕ ⓘ The town was developed by the Victorians when the railway arrived. Tourist attractions include Oban Distillery, The Highland Discovery Centre, 'A world in Miniture', McCaig Museum, and the glassworks.

Dunstaffnage Castle The Stone of Destiny was used here in 844 for Kenneth MacAlpin's coronation, before being taken to Scone.

The minor roads to the east, including the Glen Lonan road have a rolling, 'back-alley' feel, twisting through moorland and picturesque, wooded hills. In contrast the A85 from Connel to Taynuilt is lined with a succession of wooded, Baronial-style

27

estates. It is quite unpleasant to cycle on.

▲   Oban (01631) 562025
△   Jeremy Inglis, 21 Airds Crecent, Oban
        (01631) 565065
        Oban Backpackers Lodge, Breadalbane Street, Oban
        (01631) 562107/563323
🚲   D. Graham, Combie St., Oban (01631) 562069
        Oban Cycles, Craigard Rd, Oban (01631) 566996

Arduaine, near Oban: Photo. Tim Hughes

Islay

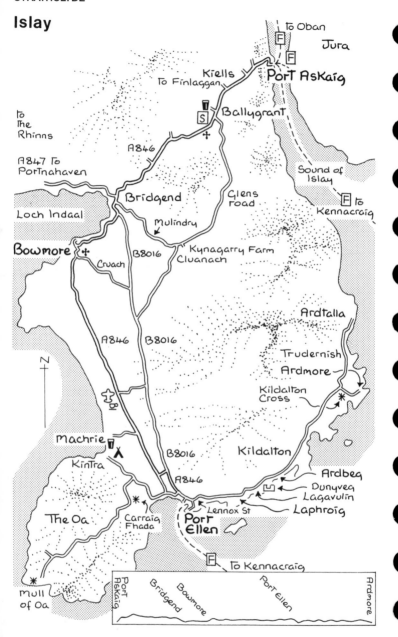

ISLAY (ILE)

Port Askaig – Bowmore – Port Ellen	**19 miles**
Bridgend – Portnahaven	**14 miles**
Port Ellen – Ardmore	**8 miles**

The 'green isle', pronounced 'Ila', and not, as one time resident Donovan sang, rhyming with hay. The Hebridean islands are always interesting, but Islay is attractive too. The climate is mild enough to grow crops, the barley spawning the island's eight distilleries, though nowadays the grain is imported.

Cycling is a real pleasure on Islay with the variety, although not infinate, definately avoiding the stale, and the absence of car-borne tourists is a big bonus. It is renown for its birdlife, with over 180 recorded species, including the shy Corncrake. Improved grassland has attracted large numbers of overwintering Barna-cle Geese, for which some farmers are compensated to allow them to graze. Others are not, and, as geese do not respect boundaries, this is a bone of some contention.

Islay teems with prehistoric remains. There are three ancient crosses and the remains of two important stongholds, the chief seats of the MacDonalds. It has also its fair share of deserted villages. The population of 15,000 in 1831 has, by emigration, been reduced to less than 4000 today, many of whom are non-gaelic incomers, and job opportunities remain scarce. As the local leaning on the hotel bar said to the barmaid in October, 'for the next six months it's just you on that side and me on this'.

The South

Port Ellen (Port Eilein) 🍴 ☕ Ⓢ Despite being the largest centre of population on the island, it has an air of time having passed it by. The village dates from 1821, and the harbour is used for the importation of grain for the distilleries. The Calmac ferry to Kennacraig (Kintyre) runs once or twice a day.

The Oa (pronounced 'oh') Once the scene of illicit distilling and smuggling, the people were shipped to the USA at the end of the last century, and sheep don't drink whisky.

At the Mull of Oa, above the sheer cliffs looking out to Rathlin Island and Antrim, stands the American Memorial, built by the

American Red Cross to commemorate the U.S. servicemen lost when the 'Tuscania' was torpedoed in February 1918.

From Port Ellen the road east kisses the castellated rocky shore, passing three white painted distilleries at Laphroaig, Lagavulin and Ardbeg.

Dunyveg Castle Built into the rock in 13c, it was one of the principle castles of the Lords of the Isles.

Kildalton Castle A ruined 19c mansion, the home of John Ramsay, whose family was cursed by one of the women he evicted and sent to America.

Kildalton High Cross One of Scotland's finest, dating from 800 AD and carved in local blue stone by an Iona sculptor. The churchyard also contains medieval graveslabs.

Trudernish Point A dun (fort) has been vitrified.

The Middle

There are two roads to Bowmore and Bridgend. The 'High Road', the B8016, was begun in 1841 to provide work during the potato famine. It runs along a line of farms, some still working, littered with rusting farm machinery. The 'Low Road' dates from 1885, also built as a 'relief' measure. It traverses the bog, passing on the way, the airport.

Bowmore (Bogh Mor) 🍴 ☕ S i A pleasant black-and-white town dominated by the Bowmore Distillery. Both town and church date from 1767, the latter built round 'so there would be no corner for the devil to hide'.

Bridgend (Beul an Atha) 🍴 S The A846 continues through a remarkably varied, well-balanced landscape to Port Askaig, passing Finlaggan.

Finlaggan ('the ancient seat of the Lords of the isles') Fangs of masonry are left of the castle of the Lords of the Isles; here they were proclaimed and held Council. A Visitor Centre tells all.

Port Askaig (Port Asgaig) 🍴 S A small settlement dominated by the 16c hotel and the ferry jetty. Western Ferries ply the

Rhinns of Islay

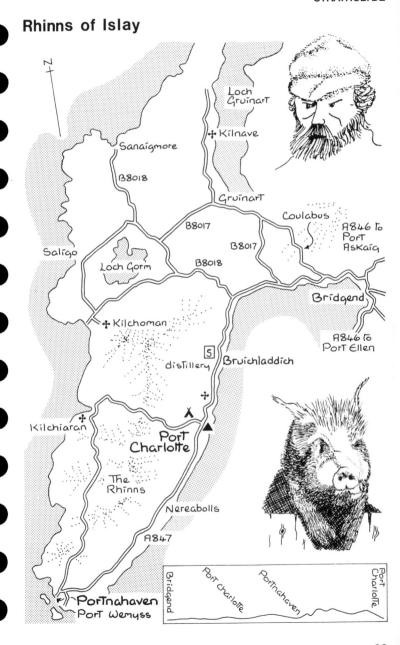

N

Loch Gruinart

✝ Kilnave

Sanaigmore

B8018

Gruinart

B8017

Coulabus

A846 to Port Askaig

B8017

Saligo

Loch Gorm

B8018

Bridgend

✝ Kilchoman

A846 to Port Ellen

5 distillery

Bruichladdich

Kilchiaran ✝

Port Charlotte

The Rhinns

Nereabolls

A847

Portnahaven
Port Wemyss

Bridgend · Port Charlotte · Portnahaven · Port Charlotte

33

Sound of Islay to Jura every hour during the day. Calmac run daily ferries to Kennacraig (Kintyre), and, once a week to Colonsay and Oban. The coast here has the smallest tidal range in Britain.

A mile to the north is the Caol Ila Distillery.

A backwoods route, along the Glens Road, takes you through the deserted heart of Islay, skirting the hills, deer forest and pine woods, and provides a contrasting alternative. It is littered with standing stones and duns.

Rhinns of Islay

The run from Bridgend to Portnahaven sweeps majestically along the shore of Loch Indaal. It hums with birdwatchers. The Rhinns is the heart of Islay's farming, serving the Port Charlotte Creamery, where a mellow cheese is produced.

Port Charlotte (Port Sgioba) ☕ 🍴 S The 'Queen of the Rhinns' is a pretty, planned village, laid out at the beginning of 19c by Rev. Malcolm Maclaurin, each house to be identical in size. Visit the Museum of Islay Life.

Portnahaven and Port Wemyss Former fishing villages, they take the brunt of the Westerlies.

'Kil' or 'Cil' means church in Gaelic. There are three on the west coast of the Rhinns to look for.

A winding, jack-in-a-box road goes north from Portnahaven to Kilchiaran and a roofless, but restored chapel, said to have been founded by St Columba.

A long detour must be undertaken, cycling through Port Charlotte to reach Kilchoman. Here a beautiful 14c Celtic cross was erected by John, first Lord of the Isles, in memory of his second wife. At the base is a wishing stone, to be turned by expectant mums hoping for a son. A white cross nearby commemorates the dead on HMS 'Otranto', torpedoed off this coast in 1918.

Cycle back past Loch Gorm, with its stump of castle ruins and, in winter, huge numbers of Barnacle, Greylag and Greenland White-Fronted Geese, to the head of loch Gruinart, scene of a bloody MacDonald/MacLean battle, and up to Kilnave. Here is the island's third cross, pure Celtic, dating from AD 750, but much worn.

▲   Port Charlotte (01496) 850385
△   Kintra Bunkbarns/Hostel, Kintra, Port Ellen
      (01496) 302051
🚲   (cycle hire) Islay Leisure, Bowmore Post Office
      (01496) 810366
      (cycle hire) Macaulay and Torrie, Port Ellen
      (01496) 302053 (hire only 'the traditional type,
      without gears')

Jura

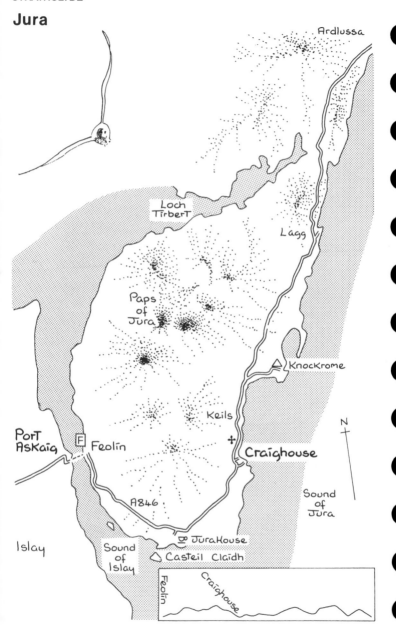

Ardlussa

Loch Tirbert

Lagg

Paps of Jura

Knockrome

Keils

N

Port Askaig

Feolin

Craighouse

A846

Sound of Jura

Islay

Sound of Islay

JuraHouse

Casteil Claidh

Feolin

Craighouse

36

JURA (DIURA)

Feolin – Lagg   16 miles

The name is from the Norse Dyr Oe (deer island). Most of Jura is broad, trackless blanket bog, home to over 5000 deer, and wild goats. Western Ferries run an hourly service during daylight hours from Port Askaig to Feolin, and from there one road tracks around to Craighouse and on to Lagg and Ardlussa. There are great views of Islay, Kintyre and over to Northern Ireland, and you will see more deer than range rovers or any other vehicles. The Paps of Jura, rising to 2571 feet, dominate the island.

The island was owned by the MacDonalds, who sold it to the Campbells of Argyll in 1607. In the late 18c it was a breeding ground for black Highland cattle, with over 1000 exported each year, supporting a population of 1300. Sheep replaced cattle, and deer replaced sheep. Less than 200 people live here now, and from September much of the island is closed for deer stalking.

Caisteal Claidh On the island of Am Fraoch Eilean are the ruins of this Norman castle, built around 1154 by Somerled to defend the Sound of Jura.

Craighouse ☕ 🍴 Ⓢ is the main village, with a steamer pier built by Telford in 1814 and the Jura Distillery, opened in 1810, enlarged in 1875, closed in 1904 and reopened in 1963. In the churchyard a stone commemorates Gillour MacCrain, who saw '180 Christmasses' before dying in 1645.

Inverlussa has the grave of another MacCrain, Mary, who died in 1856 at the comparatively young age of 126. Beyond is Barnhill, where an ageing George Orwell wrote '1984'. Beyond that, inaccessible by bike is a huge cave, Bagh Gleann nam Muc, said to be the burial place of a Norwegian prince whose galley was consumed in the Gulf of Corryveckan. The Gulf, with a tide race of up to 12 mph is presided over by the legendary 'Caillich', an old woman who decides which ships survive. St. Columba is said to have navigated it in full flood, calming the waters 'with words alone'.

△   Knockrome Bunkhouse, Knockrome, Jura
        (01496) 820332

Cowal: Dunoon and Loch Eck

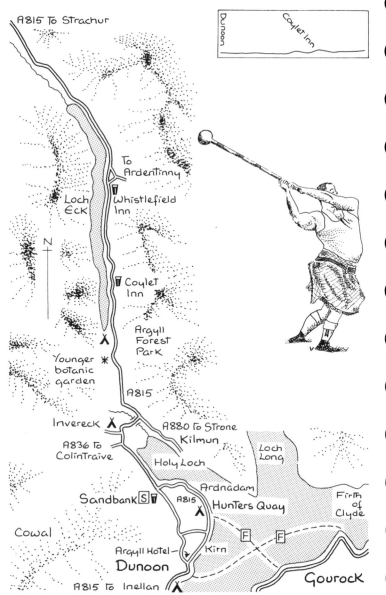

A815 To Strachur

Dunoon | Coylet Inn

To Ardentinny

Loch Eck
Whistlefield Inn

N

Coylet Inn

Argyll Forest Park

Younger botanic garden

A815

Invereck
A880 To Strone
Kilmun
A836 To Colintraive
Holy Loch
Loch Long
Ardnadam
Sandbank S
A815
Hunters Quay
Firth of Clyde
Cowal
F F
Argyll Hotel
Kirn
Dunoon
A815 To Inellan
Gourock

COWAL : DUNOON and LOCH ECK

Dunoon – Strachur   **19 miles**

Dunoon is nothing to write home about, and the 'conurbation' straggles on until Sandbank is reached, but the run along Loch Eck is a pure delight.

Ferries. From the mainland, Western Ferries run a regular service from Cloch Point to Hunters Quay, and Calmac run a rival service from Gourock to Dunoon.

Dunoon 🍴 ☕ S ⓘ A Victorian, Clydeside resort, and yachting centre. The Cowal Games are among the largest of such gatherings.

Hunters Quay 🍴 S The first Scottish yacht club was formed here in 1856. It boasts the smallest post office in the UK, built for King George the Fifth, a keen sailor, when he stayed at the Royal Marine hotel.

Sandbank 🍴 S ☕ The former base for the US Navy's Polaris submarines, and former home to a shipyard in which America's Cup Challengers have been built.

Kilmun The church was established here by St Fintan Munn in the 6c; then a collegiate church was built in 1442, the tower of which stands beside the church of 1841. Holy Loch was so named from a shipload of soil from Jerusalem being shipped to St. Mungo's Church, Glasgow, but stranded here, and snaffled by Kilmun.

Benmore The Younger Botanic Garden has a famous avenue of redwoods, rhododendron and azaleas.

Loch Fyne

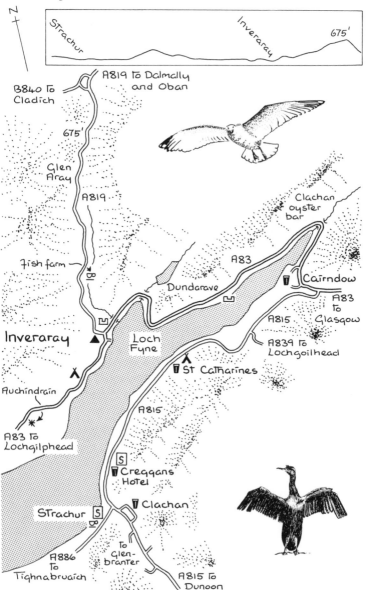

N

Strachur

Inveraray

675'

A819 To Dalmally
and Oban

B840 To
Cladich

675'

Glen
Aray

A819

Fish farm

Dundarave

Clachan
oyster
bar

A83

Cairndow

A83
To
Glasgow

A815

A839 To
Lochgoilhead

Inveraray

Loch
Fyne

St Catharines

Auchindrain

A815

A83 To
Lochgilphead

S

Creggans
Hotel

Strachur   S

Clachan

A886
To
Tighnabruaich

To
Glen-
branter

A815 To
Dunoon

40

LOCH FYNE

Strachur – Inveraray **19.5 miles**

This is a powerful land, waves of mountains roll into the distance; crashing rivers pour into sea lochs whispering with mists and midges. Unfortunately the roads are fast and open, though only the A83 has any quantity of traffic. Take care. The climb over to Loch Awe is long and gentle.

Strachur 🍴 🅂 ☕ At Creggans Inn is the site of MacPhunn's Cairn. MacPhunn of Drip was a local laird who fell on hard times and took to stealing sheep. For this he was hanged at Inveraray, and his wife, who was nursing a baby at the time, invited to collect his body. This she did by boat, but half way across Loch Fyne she saw the body move, so she mixed up some of her own milk with whisky and forced it through his lips, and, as the law did not allow him to be hanged twice, they lived happily for many years.

Dundarave Castle A 16c tower house, restored in 1911.

Inveraray 🍴 🅂 ☕ ⓘ The town retains its Georgian atmosphere, being built in 1744 by the Third Duke of Argyll who burnt the old village to make way for the present castle. The seat of the Campbells, the castle grounds are vast, thirty miles around, and over two million trees were planted, some by notables such as Tennyson and Gladstone. The castle itself, built between 1744 and 1761 contains paintings, armaments and other treasures. In the town the Jail is a must for all punishment enthusiasts (there is a souvenir shop). The Bell Tower has the world's third heaviest ring of ten bells. Further down the loch is a restored West Highland township at Auchindrain.

Glen Aray Near the summit is a memorial to Neil Munro, novelist and author of the 'Para Handy' stories. The Glen is said to be haunted by a company of redcoats on the march.

▲ Inveraray (01499) 2454
🚲 (cycle hire) Strachur Filling Station, Strachur
(01369) 860227

Loch Awe and Loch Etive

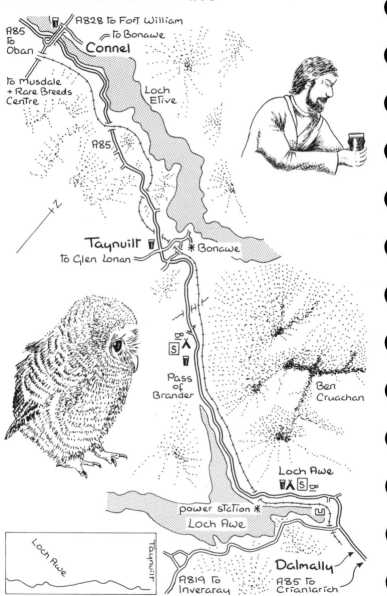

A85 To Oban

A828 to Fort William

to Bonawe

Connel

to Musdale + Rare Breeds Centre

Loch Etive

A85

Taynuilt

to Glen Lonan

Bonawe

Pass of Brander

Ben Cruachan

Loch Awe

power station
Loch Awe

Dalmally

A819 to Inveraray

A85 to Crianlarich

Loch Awe

Taynuilt

42

LOCH AWE and LOCH ETIVE

Inveraray – Taynuilt   **24 miles**

At 3611 feet Ben Cruachan dominates this stretch, together with the impressive Loch Awe (freshwater) and Loch Etive (salt). The scale is huge and the cyclist can feel vulnerable. On those mornings with a fuzzy head and aching legs the adversaries mount up; the elements, the campervans, the midges, the mighty bowls of porridge.

Dalmally The village grew in the 1880's, around the West Highland Railway, and is now known for its angling, sheep market and shinty pitch.

Kilchurn Castle A MacGregor stronghold before the Campbells took it over, following Bruce's victory in the Pass of Brander.

Cruachan Power Station opened in 1965, costing £24m. It became the most powerful generating station in Scotland. It operates on a pump storage system, with a cavern inside the mountain carved out, as large as St Pauls's Cathedral.

Pass of Brander Here both Wallace and Bruce fought victorious battles against English allies.

Taynuilt 🍺 Ⓢ Following the Jacobite defeat a number of charcoal burning ironworks were built in the Highlands to utilise the vast Caledonian forests. The most complete is here, at Bonawe. Established in 1753 the furnace could make 700 tons of iron a year, for which it required 3,500 tons of wood. Canon balls used at Trafalgar and Waterloo were made here. Sheep ensured that the forest never regenerated.

LINK Section : Ardrossan - Kilbirnie

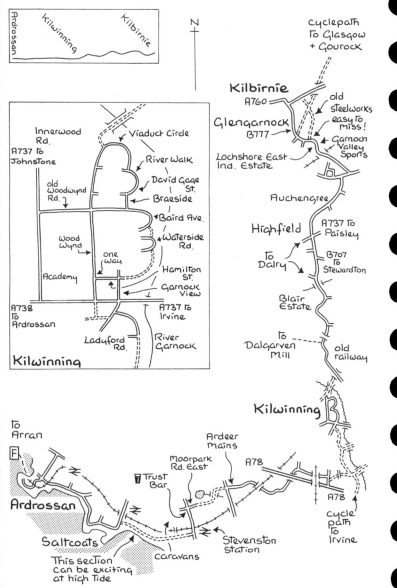

LINK SECTION : ARDROSSAN – KILBIRNIE

Ardrossan – Kilbirnie   **15 miles**

This section is included to complete the 'Argyll' loop, and because, in really bad weather the Arran ferry to Ardrossan sometimes puts in further up the coast. The A78 coast road is shorter, but becomes most unpleasant for cycling as the traffic increases north of Largs. Instead the cyclist should use the Irving Railway Path and Cycle Route, which forms part of Sustrans' National Cycle Network. The cycle path is waymarked, but signs do go missing, and care is needed in places to stay on the route. All support for Sustrans is welcome: Sustrans, 53 Cochrane St,. Glasgow, G1 1HL. tel (0141) 552 8241

Much of Ayrshire is a 'subrural' environment, a contradictory blend of pleasant, undulating farmland, and people desperately trying to carve a living out of the skeletons of the past.

Ardrossan 🚉 Ⓢ ☕ Laid out in 1806 to serve the harbour.

Stevenson and Saltcoats 🚉 Ⓢ ☕ Developed at the end of the 17c with a coal mine and harbour for its export. These are grey, cementy sort of places.

Kilwinning 🚉 Ⓢ The Abbey ruins date from the 13c. Dalgarven Mill is an early 17c flour mill, holding the Ayrshire Museum of Countryside and Costume.

🚲 AMG Cycles Ltd, Saltcoats (01294) 463421
Irvine Cycles (01294) 272712
Tam's Car and Cycle, Kilwinning (01294) 557258
RT Cycles, Glengarnock (01505) 682191
Davidson Sports, Irvine (01294) 313332

LINK Section: Kilbirnie - Gourock

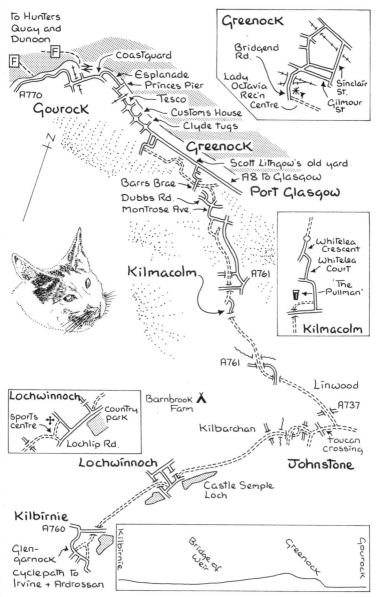

To Hunters Quay and Dunoon

F F

A770

Gourock

Coastguard
Esplanade
Princes Pier
Tesco
Customs House
Clyde tugs

Greenock

N

Scott Lithgow's old yard
A8 to Glasgow

Port Glasgow

Barrs Brae
Dubbs Rd.
Montrose Ave.

Greenock

Bridgend Rd.

Lady Octavia Rec'n Centre

Sinclair St.

Gilmour St.

Kilmacolm

A761

Whitelea Crescent

Whitelea Court

'The Pullman'

Kilmacolm

A761

Linwood

A737

Barnbrook Farm

Lochwinnoch

Sports Centre

Country park

Lochlip Rd.

Kilbarchan

Toucan Crossing

Johnstone

Lochwinnoch

Castle Semple Loch

Kilbirnie

A760

Glengarnock

Cyclepath to Irvine + Ardrossan

Kilbirnie

Bridge of Weir

Greenock

Gourock

46

LINK SECTION : KILBIRNIE – GOUROCK

Kilbirnie – Gourock **26 miles**

The cycle path is more heavily used towards Paisley. Packs of day-glo helmeted toddlers just out of stabilisers fly about like pinballs, and ingenuity is required in making the required warning sounds when approaching pedestrians from behind. If you don't know any choice Glaswegian invectives, try whistling 'Flower of Scotland'. At Greenock there is a swift descent to urban pandemonium, with the all-pervading smell of curry, and a truly amazing backdrop across the Clyde.

Kilbirnie ⊺ Ⓢ The town prospered from its large steelworks, now razed to the ground.

Kilbarchan An 18c handloom weaving centre; a weavers cottage has been preserved.

Kilmacolm A well heeled residential centre for the Glasgow conurbation since the 19c.

Greenock ⊺ Ⓢ ☕ In the late 18c it became the deep-water port for Glasgow. Badly damaged by German bombs in the 1939-45 war, many fine victorian buildings survive, including the Municipal Buildings and Customs House. On Lyle Hill, above the town, stands a huge granite Cross of Lorraine, a memorial to the 'Free French' who used Greenock in the same war.

Gourock ⊺ Ⓢ ☕ Ⓘ Half port, half resort and half neither. Two ferries ply the Clyde to Cowal, Calmac from Gourock Pier, and Western Feries from a mile further on.

🚲   Tortoise Cycle Centre, Johnstone (01505) 335551
Aerobikes Cycle Co, Greenock (01475) 888900
Halfords Ltd., Greenock (01475) 781444
J. S. Phillips, Greenock (01475) 726322

Roads to the Isles

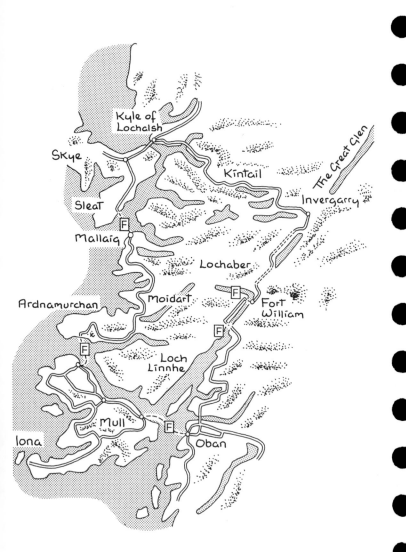

ROADS TO THE ISLES

Ironically, the much publicised 'Road to the Isles', the A830 from Fort William to Lochailort and on to Mallaig, has not been included in this book. There is nothing wrong with it , except for the coaches and caravans in summer, just as there is nothing wrong with the A851 from Corran Ferry through Ardgour and Sunart to Ardnamurchan. The more interesting cycling is along the seaward edge from Oban; over to Mull, back across to Ardnamurchan, through Moidart and Arisaig, crossing over to Skye and reaching Kyle of Lochalsh via the Sleat district of Skye.

The return half of the 'loop' gives a taste of the raw scale of the Western Highlands, crossing the mountain passes in Kintail before dropping into the Great Glen, and working back via the Great Glen Cycle Route and minor roads where possible to Oban.

There are more alternatives in this area than the rest of the Western Highlands. It pays to do a little pouring over the map before you set out, especially if you are considering using the railheads at Oban, Mallaig and Kyle of Lochalsh.

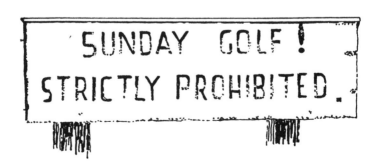

Mull

MULL (MUILE)

Sixty million years ago molten matter erupted through volcanoes, whose eroded summits and lava flows now form the islands of Mull, Skye, Rhum, Canna, Muck and Eigg. The igneous rocks which form Mull are complicated and have left us with large lava beds, pink granite and basalt cliffs, including columnal basalt at Staffa.

The clearances hit Mull particularly hard, the population declining from around 10,000 in 1821 to less than 1,600 today, and still falling. In recent times much of the island has been heavily planted by the Forestry Commission to fuel the pulpmill at Fort William.

The main ferry, from Oban to Craignure runs 5 to 7 times a day all week, all year. Five miles up the coast a regular ferry plies between Fishnish and Lochaline (Morvern), and a small vehicular ferry runs from Tobermory to Kilchoan (Ardnamurchan) 6 times a day (Sundays only in July and August).

As can be seen from the adjoining map, the cyclist on Mull has a choice of route.

Eastern Mull

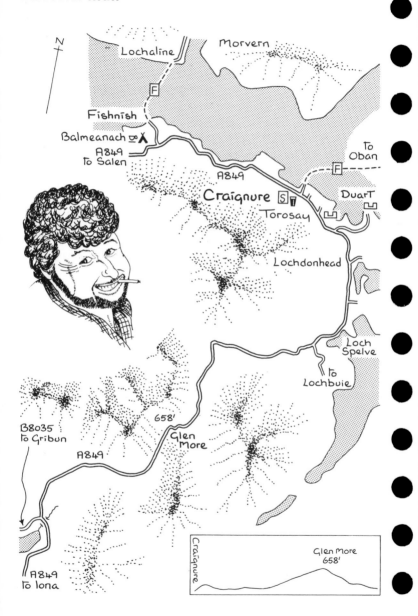

N

Lochaline Morvern

F

Fishnish

Balmeanach ⌂ ✗

A849
To Salen

A849

Craignure S 🏨 Duart

Torosay

To Oban

F

Lochdonhead

Loch
Spelve

To
Lochbuie

658'

Glen
More

B8035
To Gribun

A849

A849
To Iona

Craignure · Glen More 658'

EASTERN MULL

Craignure – Pennyghael   **18.5 miles**

On the ferry from Oban the boat squeezes between Lismore, to the north, and Lady's Rock, to the south. The former, for many years, housed the only other Christian Centre in the Highlands, Viking raiders having destroyed the more northerly monasteries, leaving Iona and the monastery of St Moluag on Lismore. Here a cathedral was established in the 13c, but burned to the ground during the Reformation. Lady's Rock, on the other hand, was where, in 1523, Lachlan of Duart exposed his Campbell wife to be drowned by the rising tide so that he could marry a local wench. Somehow, these two places symbolise much of the island of Mull.

Craignure 🍴 S ☕ i Cycling South

Torosay A victorian pile with fine gardens and a miniture railway.

Duart Castle The dramatic 13c keep, restored in 1911/12 and built on an even older castle, is the home of the rich and powerful MacLeans of Duart.

Glen More The A849 runs south, then west towards Iona. As it passes Loch Spelve it is joined by a track from Port nam Marbh (the Haven of the Dead), the route taken by the illustrious dead, who hereby keep you company to Iona.
Glen More is gloomy and windswept, and full of tales of blood and gore, including that of a fierce dragon lured to its death, and the story of Euan of the Little Head, whose ghost still roams. Euan, or Eoghann a' Chin Bhig, was a harbinger of disaster for the MacLeans of Loch Buie, for, when mortal, he was egged on by his wife to rise against his powerful father. Euan, riding recklessly into the attack, had his head cut off, and his horse returned with his headless body. Watch out!

Craignure – Cycling North

Going north, things are not so gloomy, the island roads are more peaceful than those on the mainland, and the views over the Sound of Mull are excellent.

Fishnish The Sound is crossed by the Fishnish – Lochaline ferry. This was the site of an ancient drovers fair.

Southern Mull

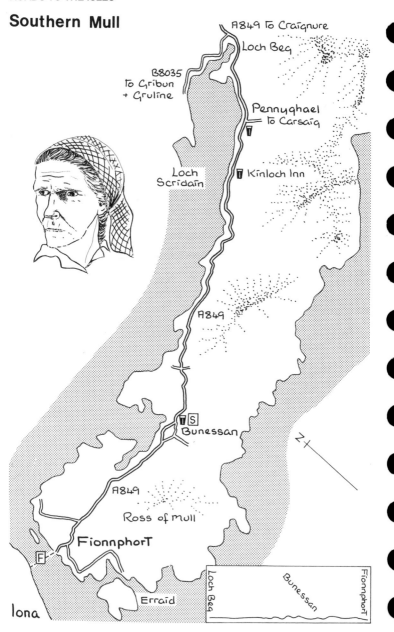

A849 To Craignure

Loch Beg

B8035
To Gribun
+ Gruline

Pennyghael
To Carsaig

Loch
Scridain

Kinloch Inn

A849

Bunessan

N

A849

Ross of Mull

FionnphorT

F

Iona

Erraid

Loch Beg	Bunessan	FionnphorT

SOUTHERN MULL

Pennyghael – Fionnphort **14.5 miles**

The road to Iona follows the coast around Loch Scridain into the Ross of Mull. This area has fewer estates than the rest of the island, and, consequently, more crofting. It is also rich in standing stones and stone circles.

Fionnphort 🍴 ☕ S This neat village with its wonderful white-sanded bay, is often heaving with visitors and pilgrims on their way to Iona. A huge car park contains the vehicles that have belted past you for the last few hours. Calmac operates a half-hourly ferry service from here to Iona.

To the south is the island of Erraid, the inspiration for R.L. Stevenson's 'Kidnapped'. He came from a lighthouse-building family, and Erraid was a lighthouse 'mecca'.

To the north is an area of pinkish granite, which, when quarried, was used to build Blackfriars Bridge and the Albert Memorial in London.

Iona

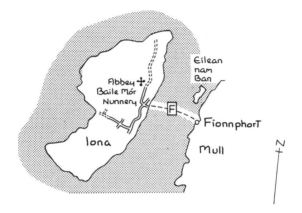

Tobermory, Mull: Photo. David Paterson

Arriving on Iona: Photo. David Paterson

Ullapool Harbour: Photo. David Paterson

Loch Eilt, Moidart: Photo. David Paterson

St Martin's and St John's Crosses, Iona: Photo. David Paterson

IONA (I CHALUIM CHILLE OR I)

Iona is not spectacular, but it is the premier shrine in Scotland, and a place of pilgrimage, with up to half a million visitors a year. In Gaelic the island was Innis nan Druinich ('Isle of the Druidic Hermits'), a place of worship before St columba arrived in AD 563. St Columba was already well established in Ireland, but a misjudgment caused a bloody battle, and he left, choosing Iona to launch his missionary zeal on 'Alba', in the process establishing the Kingdom of Dalriada as supreme in Scotland (see Dunadd near Lochgilphead).

The Abbey of St Mary has an austere beauty. It was a medieval building, restored in 15c, and rebuilt this century.

The Iona Community was founded in 1938 as an experimental group of ministers and laymen dedicated to studying contemporary world problems and the role of the church.

A visitor will also find:
- 10c St Martins Cross
- Chapel of St Columba's Shrine
- 11c Relig Oran, the burial place of 48 Scottish Kings, including Macbeth and Duncan, and several Irish, Norse and French monarchs.
- 13c Nunnery
- the Well of Eternal Youth, in which women should bath before sunrise, and the Well of the North Wind, where sailors made an offering to raise a wind.

In the bay is Eilean nam Ban, the Isle of Women, to which St Columba banished the women from Iona. He was not particularly friendly towards women. 'Where there is a cow there will be a woman. And where there is a woman there will be mischief'. Hmmm!

There are boat trips from Iona to Staffa and Fingals Cave, and from Oban to Iona and Staffa.

Western Mull

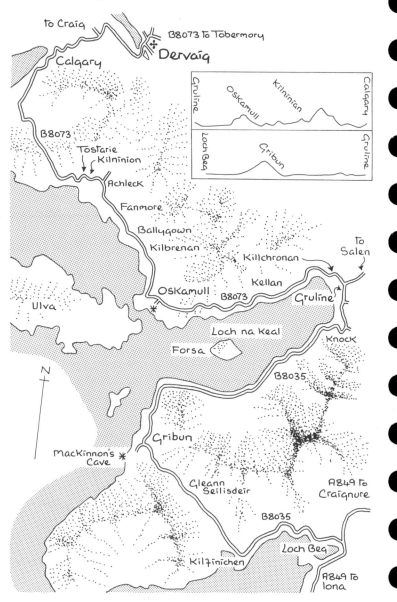

WESTERN MULL

Pennyghael junc. – Gruline	**17miles**
Gruline – Dervaig	**22.5 miles**

The run around the Western coast of Mull; Loch Scridain; Loch na Keal and Loch Tuath, is the best on the island if you are looking for breathtaking scenery rather than signs of life. Gleann Seilisdeir is a 450 feet climb among pine trees, with the brooding mass of Ben More (3169 feet) inland.

Gribun About a mile around the coast, off the road, is MacKinnon's Cave, large and deep, but accessible only at low tide. MacKinnon was a piper guiding a party around the cave. What befell them is not known, but the only survivor was a hairless dog.
Further into the wilderness of Ardmeanach is MacCulloch's Tree, a fossilised tree, 40'wide and 5'broad embedded in the lava.
The coastal road north is a grim, shadowed world, under 1000 foot high, crumbling cliffs. One of the boulders lies on the ruins of a cottage in which were lying a shepherd and his wife on their honeymoon night.

Knock lies just to the north of the centre of a double volcano which rose to a height of 8/9000 feet, 50/60 million years ago.
The road from Gruline to Calgary is outstanding, but sad, for the whole area was cleared. Offshore is Ulva. The 1840 population of 800 was reduced to 200 in the following 10 years. It is now a 'private' island, with a visitors centre.

Oskamull On the shore opposite is a cross, the grave of a daughter, immortalised many years after her death, by a tutor at Calgary. He was Thomas Campbell, and wrote a poem to 'Lord Ullin's Daughter'. She was trying to elope with the son of the Chief of Ulva, but the pair chose a treacherous crossing on a stormy night, and both perished.

Calgary All along the shore are deserted townships. East and West of the pier at Calgary were the villages of Arin and Innie Vae, cleared by the estate in 1822. Calgary, Alberta, was not named by emigrants from here, but by Colonal McLeod, remembering his youthful days on Mull with the Laird of Calgary.

Central Mull

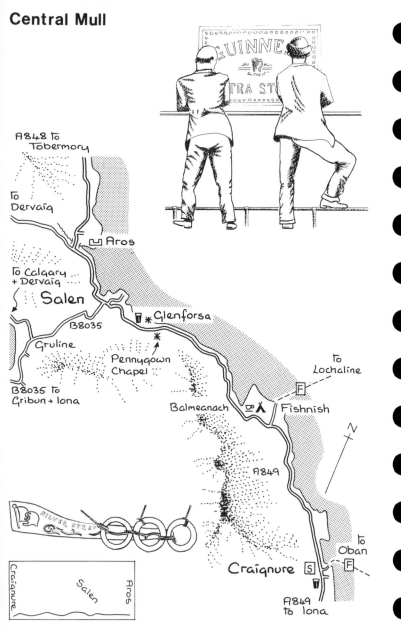

A848 To Tobermory

To Dervaig

Aros

To Calgary + Dervaig

Salen

B8035

Gruline

B8035 To Gribun + Iona

Glenforsa

Pennygown Chapel

Balmeanach

A849

To Lochaline

Fishnish

N

To Oban

Craignure

A849 to Iona

SILVER SPRAY

Craignure — Salen — Aros

CENTRAL MULL

Craignure – Aros   **12 miles**

Pennygown Chapel One of the 14 or 15 pre-Reformation chapels built on Mull by the missionaries of Iona. This is 12c, with a broken Celtic cross. Outside the chapel are two very old graveslabs belonging to an early MacLean of Duart and his wife, accused of dabbling in witchcraft, including the roasting of cats to summon the devil. It is worth remembering, as you cycle round the island that, up to the 17c, when alleged witches were burned at the stake, their internment at crossroads was considered an act of compassion by the church, which, denying them access to holy ground, held that a crossroads was the next best thing.

To the south, in Glenforsa, Mr Campbell Paterson, an Oban banker, replaced the 34 families living there in the early 19c, with 20,000 sheep.

To the north, Glenforsa hotel was imported, prefabricated in wood, from Norway, and overlooks the airstrip, built in 1966 as an army exercise.

Scalen (An't Sailean) S̲ 🍷 Lachan MacQuarrie, the 'Father of Australia', on retirement from his governorship of New South Wales, founded the village with 16 crofts in 1808.

A mile to the north is Dal na Sassunach (the Field of the Englishman), the Mull showground, so called because a sailor abandoned here in 1609 became as good a piper as MacArthur himself, and for this he was murdered here.

Aros Castle A ruin, built, like Duart, by the Kings of the Isles, one of four castles in the Sound of Mull, between which beacon signals were flashed to warn of impending trouble. It was last used in 1608 when the Viceroy of James the Fourth held court over the great Hebridean chiefs. They were all well dined, then arrested and held in Edinburgh Castle, being released only after agreeing to reforms over the rule of the Hebrides. The Lords of the Isles, an alliance under MacDonald of Islay, pursued a running battle for centuries with the Scottish monarch and Parliament, stemming from the earlier spurning of Donald Bane in favour of Robert the Bruce.

🚲 On yer Bike, Salen (01680) 300501

Northern Mull

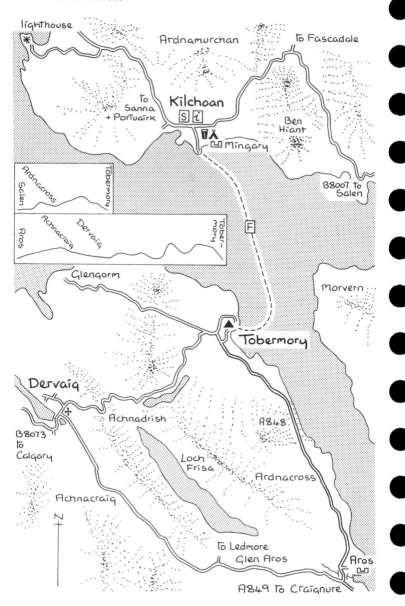

lighthouse

Ardnamurchan

To Fascadale

To Sanna + Portuairk

Kilchoan

S i

T X

Mingary

Ben Hiant

B8007 To Salen

Ardnacross

Tobermory

Salen

Aros

Achnacraig

Dervaig

Tober-mory

Glengorm

Morvern

F

Tobermory

Dervaig

Achnadrish

B8073 To Calgary

A848

Loch Frisa

Ardnacross

Achnacraig

N

To Ledmore Glen Aros

Aros

A849 To Craignure

NORTHERN MULL

Aros – Tobermory   **8 miles**
Dervaig – Tobermory   **7 miles**

The road from Dervaig to Tobermory is a dancing, dodging route with two climaxes over 500 feet, and fabulous views. On the outskirts of Tobermory it passes the site of the Poorhouse, built in 1862 to accomodate 140 people rendered destitute by the Clearances.

Dervaig S T ☕ The village was built in 1799 by MacLean of Coll, who nearly bankrupted himself countering the 'clearances' mentality, by rehousing his tenants. Unfortunately, 50 years later the Quinish Estate came into the possession of James Forsyth, who cleared his land of people with vigour. Visit the Old Byre Folk Museum. The Mull Little Theatre is the smallest in Britain.

The main road from Salen to Tobermory is steep, winding and single track. The wind whistles in the telegraph wires, and the views over the Sound of Mull, with its yachts and ferries, are stunning. An alternative is the quiet 'Glen' road up Glen Aros, with little to disturb the peace but the ruins of two villages overlooking the boglands of Glenbellert.

Tobermory T S ☕ i Established in 1789 by the British Society for Encouraging Fisheries, the town has become the centre of the island, a tourist and yachting centre, HQ of the Western Isles Yacht Club, and home to the only Bank on Mull. Tobermory means 'The Well of St Mary', and the remnants of the Chapel of St Mary contain a tombstone cracked by a late 19c bullet, fired at a grave robber. Graves had to be watched for a few weeks after burial, for the Glasgow Medical School was said to pay £5 a body. We don't have such qualms about medical science these days.

In 1588 a Spanish galleon was blown up 300 yards off MacBraynes pier. There are different stories as to who did the deed, including the possibility of an accident caused by an army of savage fairy cats (see 'The Tobermory Treasure' by Alison MacLeay). The bay is reputed to be awash with gold.

Glengorm The house was built in 1860. The name means 'Blue

Glen', a reference to the smoke from burning homesteads. Nearby is Dun Urgibul, a vitrified fort, built from silica-bearing rocks, which either deliberately or by enemy action, became fired with wood and fused together like glass.

▲ Tobermory (01688) 302481

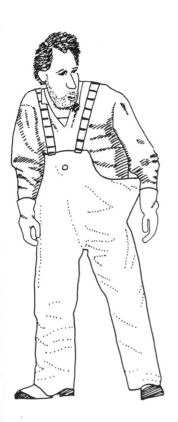

THE CALEDONIAN FOREST

Mankind's most dramatic act in the Highlands has been the destruction of the ancient Caledonian forest, of which only tiny remnants remain. Charcoal layers indicate great forest fires, probably at the time of the Viking occupation (AD 800-1100), and then, in the early 16c, the forests were discovered by lowland Scots and the English. The oaks were burned in iron smelters, the birch used for bobbins and the bark for tanning sails and ropes.

The Scottish blackface sheep was introduced in the 18c, and continued grazing by sheep and deer has prevented regeneration. The calls of the two German wars this century finished off most of the rest. The habitat destruction has brought about the disappearance of the brown bear, reindeer, elk, beaver, wild boar, wild ox, wild ponies and wolves, plus a great range of bird life.

In 1919 and 1945 there were calls for reafforestation, the Forestry Commission was established, and huge areas replanted with commercial conifer forests. By the mid-1980's, the Commission controlled nearly 10% of Scotland's land surface, by which time a large number of absentee landlords, from Pension Funds to Popstar, had joined in the blanket afforestation with Sitka spruce and Lodgepole pine. Grants and tax incentives have made such afforestation increasingly attractive, and landowners in 'sensitive' areas are even paid not to plant.

Blanket afforestation has had a major adverse effect on the ecology of the highlands and moors and continues to ruin the landscape. Chemicals are used on a large scale to deter major predators such as the pine beauty moth and the great spruce bark beetle. The promised employment benefits have not occured, and most forestry work offers an unreliable income for contractors.

A movement to reafforest Scotland with indigenous trees is growing, but it is minute in comparison to the commercial forestry industry.

Beach at Morar, Mallaig: Photo. David Paterson

ARDNAMURCHAN

This name means 'Point of the Great Ocean', and the lighthouse marks the most westerly point in mainland Britain. According to the poet Alasdair MacLean, Ardnamurchan is 'a long peninsula of solid rock, upholstered every year in threadbare green'. Geologically it forms part of the ancient volcanic activity centred on Mull, with a volcanic centre near Achnaha producing rings of Gabbro.

The Calmac ferry crosses regulary from Tobermory (£2.90 in 1996 plus £1 for the bike), and the cyclist is faced with a high-level run around Ben Hiant, then a brilliant coastal run to Salen.

Kilchoan S T i A crofting settlement. Lady cyclists should beware of offers of marriage.
Mingary Castle. Dating from the 13c, it was the seat of the ancient Lords, the MacLeans of Ardnamurchan. It was last inhabited in 1819.

Ardnamurchan and Moidart

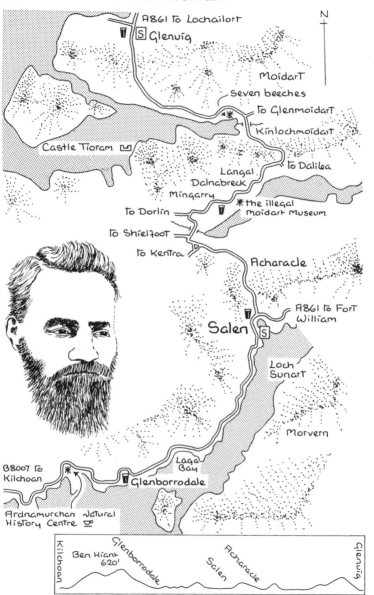

A861 To Lochailort

Glenuig

Moidart

Seven beeches

To Glenmoidart

Kinlochmoidart

Castle Tioram

To Dalilea

Langal

Dalnabreck

Mingarry

To Dorlin

the illegal Moidart Museum

To Shielfoot

To Kentra

Acharacle

A861 To Fort William

Salen

Loch Sunart

Morvern

B8007 To Kilchoan

Laga Bay

Glenborrodale

Ardnamurchan Natural History Centre

Kilchoan · Ben Hiant 620' · Glenborrodale · Salen · Acharacle · Glenuig

68

ARDNAMURCHAN AND MOIDART

Kilchoan – Kinlochmoidart   27 miles

Ben Hiant ('the Holy Mountain') As the B8007 reaches the coast, traces can be seen of the deserted townships of Bourblaig, Skinaid and Corryvulin, from which 39 families were cleared in 1828 by John MacColl to make way for sheep.
On the coast is the Cladh Chiarain, the Graveyard of Ciaran, a tall pillar of reddish stone of great age, carved with a cross and a dog.

Glenborrodale This castle was built in 1902 by Charles Rudd. During the last war it became a naval base, as Loch Sunart was a convoy assembly point.

Laga Bay The farm steadings here were built by Lord Trent, son of the founder of Boots Pure Drug Company. It then became the centre of the MacConnel Salmon Fishing operation.

Acharacle A crofting community, but, in 1838 it was home to 2000 people. Charles Rudd, having made a vast fortune in Africa, moved here and bought up much of Ardnamurchan.

Moidart is generally given over to 'game', fishing and shooting. Cycling through it is ethereal, and boggy, but for once you can forget about the clearances and concentrate on Bonnie Prince Charlie, for Kinlochmoidart House was once the seat of the MacDonalds, perhaps the most committed of his supporters.
Castle Tioram was the 14c home of the MacDonalds of Clanranald. It was fired by Clanranald himself, after the 1715 rising, to prevent it falling into Campbell hands.
The 'Seven Beeches' commemorate 'the seven men of Moidart' who accompanied Charles from France.

69

Moidart, Arisaig and Mallaig

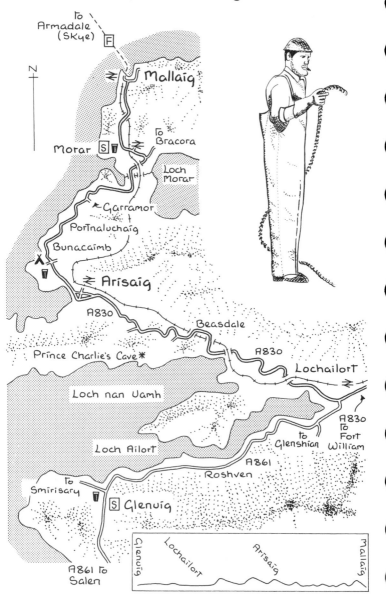

To Armadale (Skye) F

N

Mallaig

To Bracora

Morar S T

Loch Morar

H

Garramor

Portnaluchaig

Bunacaimb

Arisaig

A830

Beasdale

Prince Charlie's Cave *

A830

Lochailort

A830 To Fort William

Loch nan Uamh

to Glenshian

Loch Ailort

A861

Roshven

To Smirisary

S Glenuig

A861 To Salen

Glenuig · Lochailort · Arisaig · Mallaig

MOIDART, ARISAIG AND MALLAIG

Kinlochmoidart – Mallaig   29 miles

The run along Loch Ailort is one of those little gems that make the climbs and rain and midges worth it. Glenuig is a bustling place today, the numbers swelled hereabouts by illegal settlers.

Loch Ailort The training ground of the Special Operation Teams, the 'Odettes' and the 'Peter Churchills', who were dropped into enemy-occupied country during the last war. Belgium is like this?

Loch nam Uamh (the Loch of the Cave) The landing, and departure place of Prince Charles in 1745/6.

The Lochailort – Mallaig road is a switchback; beautiful country, but prone to bustling in summer.

Arisaig 🍴 S The bays attract yachts, and the pure white silica sand attracts trippers. Inland is a low boggy plain called the Great Moss, and between this and the sea is machair, fertile ground built up by a combination of sand and bog.

Loch Morar At 1,017 feet deep this freshwater loch is much deeper than the nearby sea. In fact the sea does not become this deep until the Continental Shelf is reached, making it the deepest water in Britain. There have been 33 sightings since 1887, of a monster called Morag.

Mallaig S 🍴 ☕ i A quirky, specialised fishing port with the harbour the centre of activity. There are too few children to keep the secondary school open, so they board during the week in Fort William.

The ferry crosses from here to Armadale (Skye), approx. 6 sailings a day. The fare in 1996 was £2.30.

△   Sheena's Backpackers Lodge, Harbour View,
        Mallaig (01687) 462764

Connel, Appin and Loch Linnhe

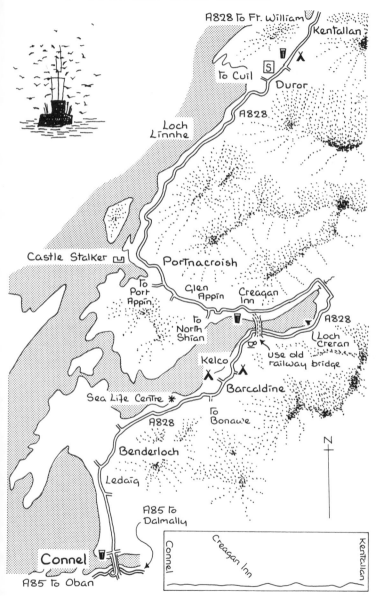

A828 To Fr. William

Kentallan

To Cuil

Duror

A828

Loch
Linnhe

Castle Stalker

Portnacroish

To
Port
Appin

Glen
Appin

Creagan
Inn

A828

To
North
Shian

Loch
Creran

use old
railway bridge

Kelco

Barcaldine

Sea Life Centre

To
Bonawe

A828

Benderloch

Ledaig

A85 To
Dalmally

Connel

A85 To Oban

Connel   Creagan Inn   Kentallan

N

CONNEL, APPIN and LOCH LINNHE

Connel – Kentallan   21 miles

You are about to cycle along the tremendous fault line of Loch Linnhe/the Great Glen, a line much inundated with sea lochs and freshwater lochs. The land to the north has slipped by approximately 65 miles.

This is a delightful, shore-lapped ride with Mull on the horizon. There is a short-cut over to Creagan Inn by pushing your bike up and over the old railway bridge.

Connel 🍴 Ⓢ Beneath the bridge are the 'Falls of Lora' a great hazard to the ferries before the bridge was converted to road traffic. They are caused by odd tidal flows. For three hours a day the tide on one side of the bridge is falling, whereas on the other side it is still ebbing.

Barcaldine The grey buildings by Loch Creran are the 'seaweed' factory, for emulsifiers and thickeners in , among other things, ice cream.

The castle (private) is an early 17c tower house, a fine example of a laird's dwelling.

Appin Stewart territory since the 14c, with Castle Stalker the stronghold. It was used as a gaol for prisoners taken in 1745, and has recently been restored as a house. Its situation is breathtaking. Nearby is the Appin Wildlife Museum.

Ballachulish, Loch Linnhe and Fort William

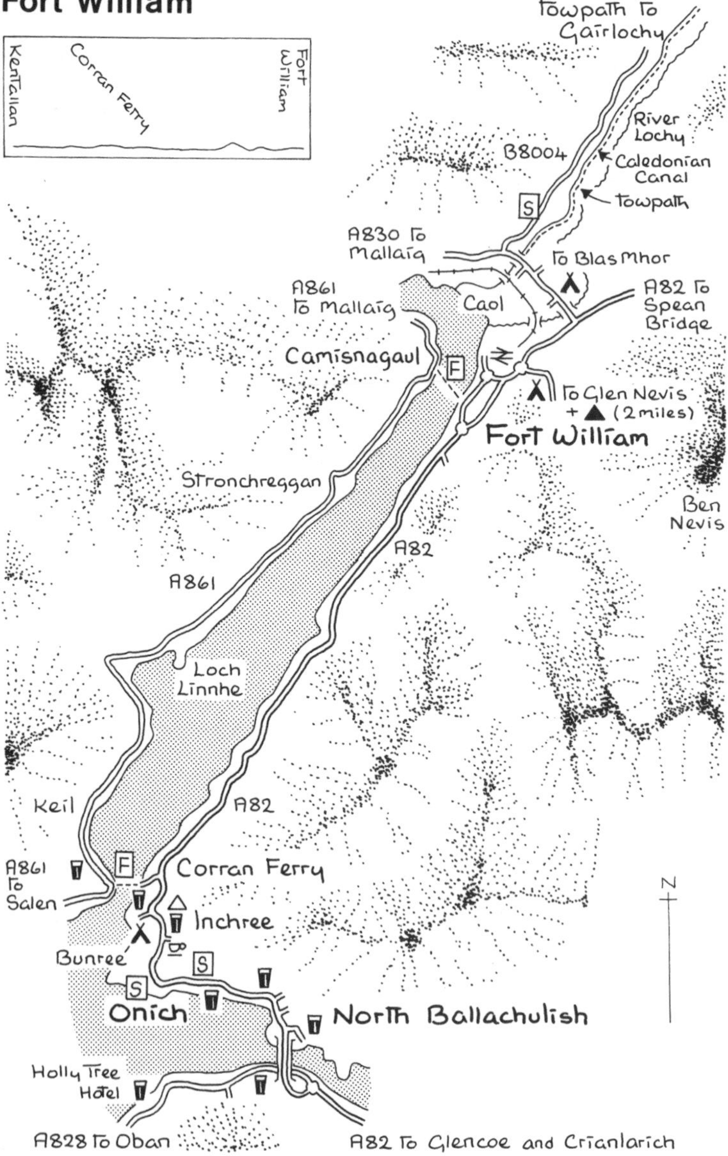

Kentallen · Corran Ferry · Fort William

Towpath To Gairlochy

B8004

River Lochy
Caledonian Canal
Towpath

S

A830 To Mallaig

To Blas Mhor

A861 To Mallaig

Caol

A82 To Spean Bridge

Camisnagaul

F

To Glen Nevis ▲ (2 miles)

Fort William

Stronchreggan

Ben Nevis

A82

A861

Loch Linnhe

Keil

A82

A861 To Salen

F

Corran Ferry

Inchree

Bunree

N

S · S

Onich

North Ballachulish

Holly Tree Hotel

A828 To Oban

A82 To Glencoe and Crianlarich

74

BALLACHULISH, LOCH LINNHE and FORT WILLIAM

Kentallan – Fort William   17.5 miles

The A82 coming down Glencoe, to Fort William and Inverness, is a pig of a road for cyclists. You can avoid it most of the time; firstly by making illegal use of the footpaths around Onich; secondly by using the peaceful, attractive A861 on the far side of Loch Linnhe; and thirdly by using the Great Glen Cycle Route.

Glencoe Two monuments bear witness to the Massacre, on Feb 13 1692, when 130 Government troops under the orders of Archibald Campbell, Tenth Earl of Argyll, slaughtered 38 MacDonalds for their tardiness in swearing allegiance to King William the Third. There is also a heather-thatched museum.

Corran Ferry takes vehicles across to the A861 on the west side of Loch Linnhe, a much more gentle road than the traffic artery, the A82. The return ferry to Fort William is from Camisnagaul, a passenger ferry (cycles carried free) operated by Highland Regional Council. It sails 5 or 6 times a day; ask for details at Corran Ferry or ring (01463) 702000

Fort William 🍴 Ⓢ ☕ ⓘ Originally called Inverlochy, the turf and wattle fort of 1650 was rebuilt in stone and named Mayburgh after the wife of King William the Third, before being named for the King himself. The Great Glen Road from Inverness to Fort William was completed in 1727 with garrisons at Inverness (Fort George), Fort Augustus and Fort William. The fort has since been demolished, and the town is a Victorian nightmare. There is the West Highland Museum to visit.

▲ Glencoe (01855) 811219
Glen Nevis (01397) 702336

△ Inchree Bunkhouse, Onich (01855) 821287
Backpackers Guest House, Alma Rd, Fort William (01397) 700711
The Smiddy Bunkhouse, Station Rd, Corpach (01397) 772467

🚲 Mountain Madness, Onich (01855) 821500
Leven Cycles, Kinlochleven (01855) 831614
Off-Beat Bikes, Fort William (01397) 704008

The Great Glen and Loch Garry

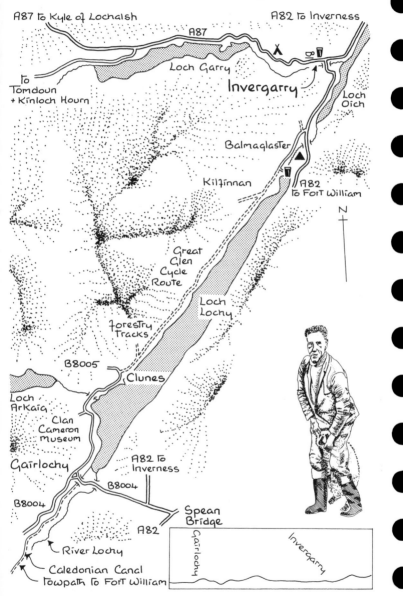

A87 to Kyle of Lochalsh

A82 to Inverness

A87

Loch Garry

Invergarry

To
Tomdoun
+ Kinloch Hourn

Loch
Oich

Balmaglaster

Kilfinnan

A82
to Fort William

N

Great
Glen
Cycle
Route

Loch Lochy

Forestry
Tracks

B8005

Clunes

Loch
Arkaig

Clan
Cameron
Museum

Gairlochy

A82 to
Inverness

B8004

B8004

Spean
Bridge

A82

River Lochy

Caledonian Canal
Towpath to Fort William

Gairlochy

Invergarry

THE GREAT GLEN, LOCH LOCHY and LOCH GARRY

Fort William – Invergarry   **23.5 miles**

The route follows the towpath of the Caledonian Canal, with magnificent views across to Ben Nevis. Minor roads to Clunes give way to forestry roads alongside Loch Lochy. These are roughish in parts, and quiet, with a feeling of isolation, with only the wind for company, and the distant hum of engines from the A82, and from cruisers plying the loch.

The Great Glen Cycle Route has been waymarked along the Great Glen, with occasional forays into the forest. The Forestry Commission have exploited this valley for two generations now, and, at minimal cost, has produced a curate's egg of a cycle route. Cyclists deserve better than these mountain climbing rough roads, eventually dissolving into an apology at the Inverness end. The best parts of the route utilise the towpath of the Caledonian Canal.

The Caledonian Canal was built 1804 to 1822, and financed largely by the government to provide a link between the North Sea and the Atlantic for the Royal Navy. It has never been commercially viable.

Invergarry 🍴 ☕ An estate village built by the Ellice family in the 1860's/ 1870's. Their crest, a mailed fist clutching a serpent can be seen above the door of the 'Inn on the Garry'.

The castle, a seat of the Macdonnells, was burnt by 'Butcher' Cumberland in 1746 for their part in helping Bonnie Prince Charlie.

Alastair Macdonnell was responsible for the 'Well of the Seven Heads', on the western shore of Loch Oich. Erected in 1812 it shows seven severed heads tied by their hair to a dirk, and marks the spot where Iain Lom Macdonnell washed the heads after taking 'ample and summary vengence' for the murder of his chief in 1663.

▲   Loch Lochy (01809) 501239

Loch Garry, Loch Cluanie and Kintail

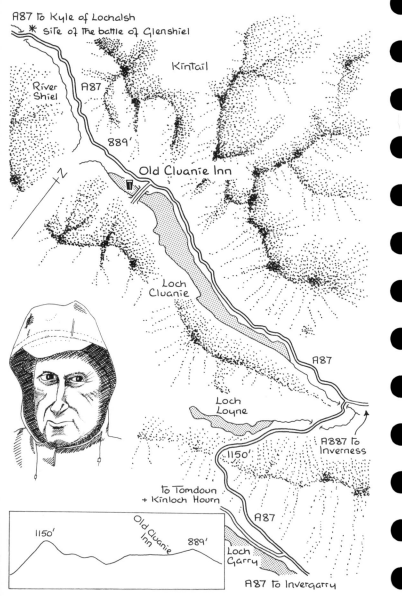

A87 To Kyle of Lochalsh

* Site of the battle of Glenshiel

Kintail

River Shiel

A87

889'

Old Cluanie Inn

N

Loch Cluanie

A87

Loch Loyne

A887 To Inverness

1150'

To Tomdoun + Kinloch Hourn

A87

Loch Garry

A87 To Invergarry

Old Cluanie Inn

1150'   889'

78

LOCH GARRY, LOCH CLUANIE and KINTAIL

Invergarry – Old Cluanie Inn   **19 miles**

This is 'big country', a mass of mountains, the pass crossing the broad backbone of Scotland. Vestiges can be seen of the old military road, built between 1750 and 1784 by Wade's successor, General Caulfeild, to link Fort Augustus with Bernera baracks at Glenelg. More recently the road crossed to Cluanie Bridge Inn on a pass reaching 1,424 feet, but improvements have reduced this to summits of 1,150' and 889'. Most of Kintail is 'under deer', and, given good cycling conditions this run can be exhilarating.

Loch Cluanie means 'the Loch of the Meadows', but the former meadows have mostly vanished following the damming of the loch for hydro-electricity.

Battle of Glensheil A monument records the site of the battle fought here in 1719 between the Redcoats and the Jacobites (see 'Eilean Donan Castle').

Morvich is the home of the Clan MacLennon Museum.

From **Sheil Bridge** i there is a alternative route to Skye. The road is much quieter than the A87, and makes use of the Glenelg -Kylerea ferry (see appendices), but the road to Glenelg crosses a steep pass above Ratagan (1,116 feet) and an equally severe pass through Glen Arroch on Skye (911 feet) !

▲   Ratagan (01599) 511243

Loch Duich and Loch Alsh

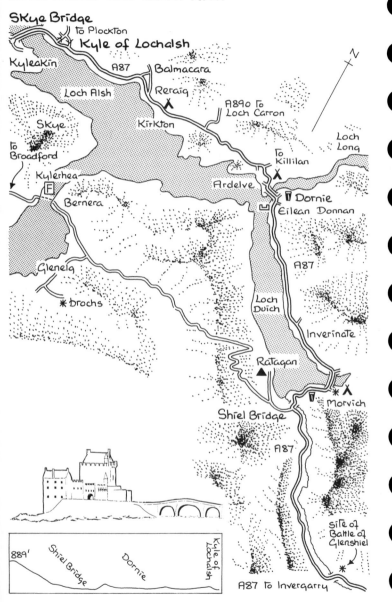

80

LOCH DUICH and LOCH ALSH

Old Cluanie Inn – Kyle of Lochalsh   **25 miles**

The 'big country' continues, and the downhill run a 'buzz' through this mass of 3000 foot peaks, down to the Lochs Duich and Alsh. For the cyclist it is a shame the road is a main one, and still being improved. The Balmacara – Kyle of Lochalsh section was built in 1970, and the Skye Bridge opened in 1996.

Dornie 🍴 Ⓢ Once a thriving fishing village, but nowadays visitors flock to see the castle on Eilean Donan. Loch Duich was named for St Dubhthach, an 11c Bishop of Ross, and Eilean Donan for the much earlier 7c Saint Donan. The existing castle, the most picturesque in the West Highlands, is a restoration of 1932 built to the plan of the 13c original, though that Norman castle was completely surrounded by water. It was built around 1230 by Alexander the Second for defence and aggression against the Norsemen who were in full occupation of Skye. His son, Alexander the Third gave it, in 1266, to Colin Fitzgerald for his services at the Battle of Largs three years earlier. Colin is thought to be the progenitor of Clan MacKenzie, whose chiefs became Lords of Kintail and Earls of Seaforth. The castle was held in the main by the wild MacRaes on behalf of the MacKenzies. After a long and bloody history, the castle's downfall came in a little known Jacobite rising in 1719. A huge supporting Spanish armada foundered off Finisterre, and a Hanoverian army under General Wightman attacked by land and sea, reducing the castle to ruins, and, in the process, ruining the MacKenzies. Their lands were forfeited and never returned.

Ardelve Here crofters from most of Lochalsh were settled in 1801 when the land was 'cleared' by Sir Hugh Innes. In Glen Udulain, for example, the Mathesons could muster 700 fighting men. No-one lives there now.

A long way up Loch Long and Glen Elchaig are the Falls of Glomach, difficult to reach, but the most spectacular waterfall in Britain.

Kyle of Lochalsh Ⓢ 🛈 🍴 ☕ The railway reached here in the 1890's, and the town grew thereafter.

ROADS TO THE ISLES

▲ Ratagan (01599) 511243
🚲 (cycle hire) Kintail Crafts, Aultachruine, Glenshiel
(01599) 511345/221
Kyle Cycles, Kyle of Lochalsh (01599) 534842

Loch Garry: Photo. David Paterson

The Hebrides

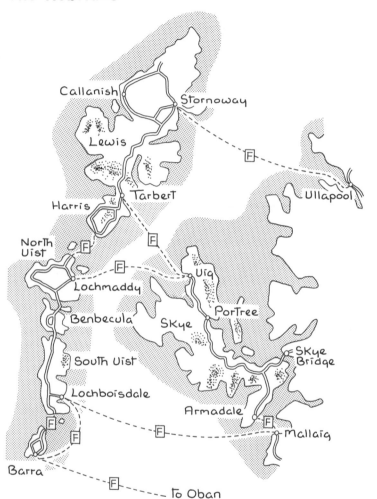

THE HEBRIDES

The name 'Hebrides' is derived from the Norse 'Havbredey', the 'Isles on the Edge of the World'. They are like nowhere else in Britain; open, wet, friendly, insular, windy and about as far removed from the urban distractions and problems of England as you can get. Even the language is different, for this is the heart of the 'Gaidhealtachd', and Gaelic (pronounced 'gallic', 'gaylic' being Irish) remains the mother-tongue. It is a lyrical and haunting speech with much throat-work, and a phraseology akin to Scandinavian languages, but, fear not, most speakers are impressively bi-lingual. Some years ago, The Western Isles Council adopted a policy of signposting place names in Gaelic, so, where appropriate, the maps have been marked bi-lingually. For the most part the Scots tongue in the Western Highlands and Islands is soft and gentle, an absolute joy to correspond with, though, just as Glaswegians have occasionally had to be dubbed for London's 'Six o'Clock News', it is sometimes difficult to tell whether the locals are speaking Gaelic or English.

Cycling The Outer Hebrides can be cycled as one route, with ferries linking the gaps. They can be reached by boat from Oban or Mallaig, by cycling across Skye to the Uig ferry, or by boat from Ullapool.

The wind is something to which the cyclist must become accustomed. When asked, a local will say 'What wind?', and tell you about a month last winter when it blew at gale force for 23 days out of 30. If there are two of you, take a tip from the racing fraternity and slipstream, it is amazing the difference it makes.

There are SYHA hostels, independent hostels and wonderfully small bothy-type hostels run by the Gatliff Trust. These are run by local people, and do not have normal hostel rules. Camping is generally permitted anywhere, except for farmland and unfriendly estates, but it invariably pays to consult the locals and ask permission where appropiate. It is also not unusual for private caravans to be let to travellers on a casual basis. Bed and Breakfast accomodation can be found everywhere, but not in such quantity as on the mainland. Hotels are few and far between. One of the great attractions for the cyclist on the islands is to escape from the throng of car-borne tourists and tourist developments. The ferries, expensive for vehicles, are a bargain for the cyclist. Pre-booking is not usually required for bikes, but, as there are often only one or two ferries a day, a phone call to check on running times is a good idea. In particular, the small ferry from the north end of Barra to South Uist, is very busy at the height of summer.

Crofting A croft has been described as 'a small piece of land surrounded by regulations'. The 1886 Crofters Act gave the crofters a good deal, though, in most cases the old croft, based on private arable land and common grazing, once considered sufficient to raise a family, is no longer economically adequate, and subsidiary employment must be found. 'Black Houses' gave way to the 'white-house', larger and healthier, erected with money earned by family members working away from home, and, more recently, with state grants and loans. The big problem is to find supplementary employment. Fishing is in decline and fish-farming is seen as a salvation despite the amount of environmental damage done to the lochs through chemicals and excessive food and faeces. There are over 18,000 crofters of whom 3,500 are on Lewis.

Religion Somewhere around the middle of Benbecula is a dividing line between the islands to the south, which are essentially Catholic, and those to the north, where the Presbyterian Free Church, the Free Church of Scotland and the Church of Scotland hold sway.

In the early 19c evangelists found fertile ground in a people economically, spiritually, politically and materially impoverished. The old ways, the song and the dancing, the games and the sports, the fiddle music and bagpipes, the pipe of tobacco and the dram of whisky, all were ruthlessly condemned as the work of the Devil. One of the institutions most sternly condemned by the Free Church ministers was the ceilidh. Cows were not milked on the Sabbath; communal singing at work and play was banished.

The new church was not welcomed by the establishment, and lay preachers gained an immense influence with huge revivalist meetings. The founding of the Free Church, known as the 'Disruption of the Church of Scotland' occurred in 1843, and even today the Free Church enjoys considerable power. On Sundays the place shuts down, with few locals out and about, except to attend church. The ministers see their responsibility extending to 'the stranger at the gate', who should be made to tow the line, though by and large foreigners are ignored.

Roots As the last of the ice sheets receded, people began to move north. The Gaelic-speaking Celts were pushed by the Anglo-Saxons, first into Ireland, and from there up the west coast of Scotland. St Columba (521-597 AD) and other Irish Saints brought a century or two of Christianity, but the Vikings came to fight and plunder, and for six centuries were the overlords of the Hebrides. Even after their departure the islands were never really incorporated into the Kingdom of Scotland, for an impressive distance separated them from the Scots-speaking rulers in the lowlands. The Islands were bypassed by the Renaissance, the Reformation penetrated only slowly, and the 1604 Union of the Crowns only distanced the Hebrides from the centres of power and prosperity.

Until the Viking period, much was forested, but a slight climatic deterioration, felling and sheep have prevented regeneration. Much is uncultivated peat bog, useful for fuel but little else. The east coast is generally uninviting and curiously dead, though the sea teems with life, fish, basking sharks, seals, otter, gannets and divers. On the west coast is the machair. Sand has blown in and countered the acidity in the peat, forming fertile soil and rich herbage. The use of seaweed as a fertiliser has nowadays largely given way to manure and chemical fertilisers, though traces can be seen of 'lazy-beds' (feannagan) in which seaweed was used on the peat to grow oats and potatoes, after they were introduced in 1752.

Barra

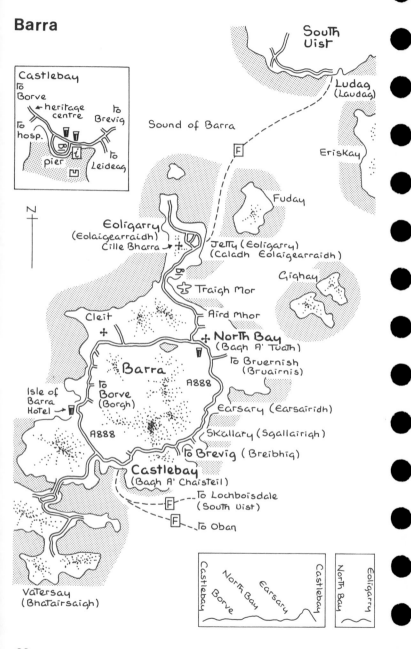

Castlebay
To Borve
← heritage centre
To Brevig
To hosp.
pier
To Leideag

N

South Uist

Ludag (Ludag)

Sound of Barra

Eriskay

Fuday

Eoligarry (Eolaigearraidh)
Cille Bharra
Jetty (Eoligarry) (Caladh Eolaigearraidh)

Gighay

Traigh Mor

Aird Mhor

Cleit

North Bay (Bagh A' Tuath)
To Bruernish (Bruairnis)

Barra

A888

To Borve (Borgh)

Earsary (Earsairidh)

Isle of Barra Hotel →

A888

Skallary (Sgallairigh)

To Brevig (Breibhig)

Castlebay (Bagh A' Chaisteil)

To Lochboisdale (South Uist)

F ... To Oban

Castlebay
Borve
North Bay
Earsary
Castlebay

North Bay
Eoligarry

Vatersay (Bhatairsaigh)

Gruinard Bay, Wester Ross: Photo. David Paterson

The empty roads of the far North West: Photo. David Paterson

The Cam Loch, with Cul Mor and Suilven: Photo. David Paterson

Cape Wrath: Photo. David Paterson

BARRA (BARRAIGH)

Castlebay – Eoligarry   10 miles

Barra is the mainlanders idea of the perfect island. It is small enough for a leisurely circuit by bike to occupy a couple of hours. The east (an Ear) coast is broken, with boats nestling in the inlets, and the west (an Lar) coast has a magnificent beach at Hallaman Bay, spoiled only by the concrete, modern hotel. In the middle is rocky moorland. The islanders speak Gaelic, and are close knit, so everyone knows everyone else's business.

Castlebay harbour has long been of strategic importance. Both warrior Celts and Norsemen settled here,and Kisimul Castle was built to defend the anchorage, as the stronghold of the MacNeil Clan in the 12c. In 1838 General Roderick MacNeil had to sell the island to pay his creditors. It was purchased by John Gordon of Cluny, a mean, rapacious man who evicted his islanders by the thousand, with a cruelty that became a national scandal. They were hunted down, and either handcuffed and forced aboard ships, or later appeared ragged and destitute in Glasgow. Colonel Gordon even offered the island to the Government as a penal colony. In 1937 Kisimul Castle was restored by the 45th Chief of Clan MacNeil, and can be visited today by boat trip.

Castlebay (Bagh A Chaisteil) 🍴 ☕ Ⓢ ⓘ A dinky town, a 19c herring port, harbouring over 400 boats at its height, replaced nowadays by lobsters and crabs. The Druid Temple has a well (Tobar-nam-Buadh, the 'Well of Virtues') which not only effects cures but also 'wards off facination'. Castlebay has the island's main harbour, and the ferry links with Oban, Mallaig and Lochboisdale (South Uist) approximately once a day.

Traigh Mor has a 'low impact' airport. It is a breeding ground for cockles, living below the old, discarded shells, though in recent years these have been removed to clad, or harl, the walls of houses, thereby disturbing the self-renewing cycle of the beach.

Eoligarry (Eolaigearraidh) A local, passenger ferry negotiates the treacherous waters to Ludag on South Uist, twice a day (£2.50/person, £2/cycle in 1996).

THE HEBRIDES

In 1941 the S.S. Politician, bound for New York with 24,000 cases of whisky, foundered off the north of Eriskay. Remains of the wreck can still be seen. Compton MacKenzie, whose book 'Whisky Galore' is based on this event, had moved to Barra in 1933, and is buried in Cille-Bharra, along with the MacNeil chieftains. Look for the 14c/15c 'sword-in-the-stone' tombstones.

△   Brevig (Breibhig) Hostel, Brevig
 Barra Cycle and Repair, 29 St Brendans Road
     (01871) 810284

Castlebay, Barra: Photo. David Paterson

South Uist

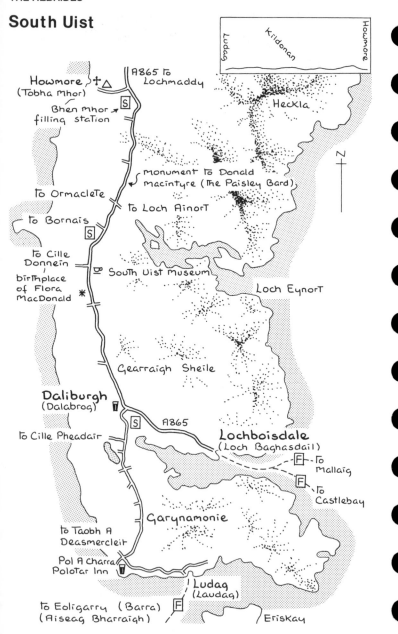

Howmore
(Tobha Mhor)

A865 to Lochmaddy

Bhen Mhor filling station

Kildonan

Ludag

Howmore

Heckla

monument to Donald Macintyre (The Paisley Bard)

To Ormaclete

To Loch Ainort

To Bornais

To Cille Donnein

South Uist Museum

Loch Eynort

birthplace of Flora MacDonald

Gearraigh Sheile

Daliburgh
(Dalabrog)

A865

To Cille Pheadair

Lochboisdale
(Loch Baghasdail)

F To Mallaig

F To Castlebay

Garynamonie

To Taobh A Deasmercleit

Pol A Charra
Polotar Inn

Ludag
(Laudag)

To Eoligarry (Barra)
(Aiseag Bharraigh)

F

Eriskay

92

SOUTH UIST (UIBHIST A DEAS)

Ludag – Howmore   **15 miles**

South Uist feels like another planet. The road spines the island, crossing watery bogs and lochs, peat-dug moors and rough farmland. To the east is a long, dark, brooding mountain mass, bristling with military hardware. To the west, homes, past and present, have been cast among the puddles, and from the low, black horizon comes the roar of the Atlantic surf. The new church at Garynamonie is almost shocking.

By the end of the 18c, fifty years of peace meant more bellies to feed from the same subsistence farming. The landowner of South Uist, MacDonald of Clanranald, discovered a demand for kelp as a source of industrial alkali, used in glass and soap works, though the process of burning the giant brown seaweed over peat fires was particularly nauseous. A workforce was essential, and the cost of the passage to the new colonies trebled to keep them here. The wages were so poor, however, that by 1811, 80% of the normal diet was potatoes. The people became dependent on kelp, so when cheaper supplies were obtained from Spain in the 1820's, it was decided that half the population (3000 people) should be shipped to the colonies. In 1841 Gordon of Cluny bought the island (see 'Barra'). He burned the houses and threw the people, bound, onto ships, chasing escapees with dogs. They were landed in Quebec with nothing to give them a fresh start. Meanwhile, back on South Uist, potato blight struck in the 1840's. The British Government, having seen the ravages of disease which followed starvation in Ireland, provided help in the form of employment. This consisted of back-breaking work making 'destitution roads' (upon which you are cycling), in exchange for a subsistence level of grain or oatmeal. The injustice was compounded by the comfortable wages paid to those administering the system, the landowners and their cronies.

Lochboisdale (Loch Baghasdail) 🍴 S ☕ i The 'centre' of South Uist. The hotel was built in 1882 along with the pier.

Howmore (Tobha Mhor) The ruins of a pre-Reformation monastery and college co-exist with the post-Reformation Presbyterian

Church, in which can be seen the surviving communion table. Between the two is the Gatliff Trust Hostel.

 Gatliff Trust, Howmore (sleeps 10) GR 757265
 Rothan Cycle Service and Repairs, Tommy MacDonald,
9 Howmore (01870) 620283/610231 (part time).

Sound of Orosay, Barra: Photo. David Paterson

South Uist and Benbecula

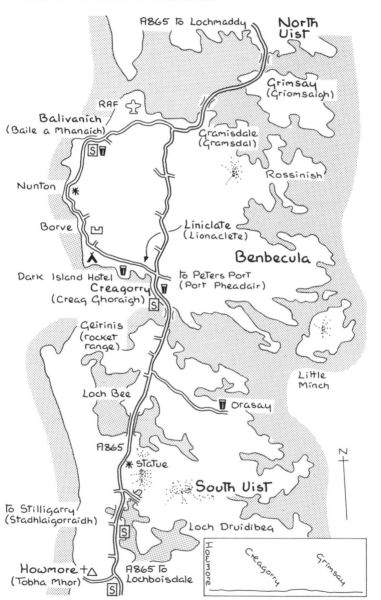

A865 To Lochmaddy

North Uist

Grimsay
(Griomsaigh)

RAF

Balivanich
(Baile a Mhanaich)

Gramisdale
(Gramsdal)

Rossinish

Nunton

Borve

Liniclate
(Lionaclete)

Benbecula

Dark Island Hotel

Creagorry
(Creag Ghoraigh)

To Peters Port
(Port Pheadair)

Geirinis
(rocket range)

Little Minch

Loch Bee

Orasay

A865

Statue

South Uist

To Stilligarry
(Stadhlaigorraidh)

Loch Druidibeg

Howmore
(Tobha Mhor)

A865 To
Lochboisdale

Howmore   Creagorry   Grimsay

SOUTH UIST and BENBECULA (UIBHIST A DEAS and BEINN A FAOGHLA)

Howmore – Grimsay   **15.5 miles**

A silvery, slippery, slivering ride to Benbecula. There, the direct route crosses a water-tickled peat-strewn moor; the coastal road follows machair with glimpses of the Atlantic and a dose of the military.

Earlier this century, reaching Benbecula was a matter of fording the sand banks, exposed at low tide, which divide it from North and South Uists. Bonnie Prince Charlie kept losing his shoes here, and making his servants retrieve them, thus slowing the pace of his retreat. The present road was built in 1983 and 1960 on narrow causeways, along which vehicles dash, inexplicably.

Loch Druidibeg A nature reserve noted for heron, geese and ferns. Work is in hand to restore a woodland on the Reserve to provide a rare habitat on the island.

Our Lady of the Isles A monumental sculpture carved by Hew Lorimer in 1957.

Loch Bee The nesting place of mute swans.

Peter's Port A pier was built at extravagant expense, though the loch mouth is practically unnavigable. It is now ruined.

Borve The castle ruins were a MacDonald home.

Nunton The ruined chapel was the centre of a pre-Reformation nunnery. A large house close by was built by the MacDonald chieftains of Clanranald after their castle at Ormaclete burned down in a moment of festivity in 1715. Here also is the grave of a mermaid killed 150 years ago by a stone thrown by a boy.

Balivanich (Baile a Mhanaich) The site of a medieval monastery was redeveloped to serve the guided missile range on South Uist, causing a 45% increase in Benbecula's population.

Rossinish From here, Bonnie Prince Charlie, disguised as maid servant Betty Burke, set sail with Flora MacDonald for Skye. (All sing together 'Speed bonnie boat, like a bird on a wing, over the sea to Skye').

Grimsay Many of the islanders take to the double-pointed lobster boats, serving the processing plant at Gramisdale.

△   Mr Millar, Bunkhouse, 22 Balivanich, Benbecula
    (01870) 602522

The debris of crofting, Benbecula: Photo. David Paterson

North Uist

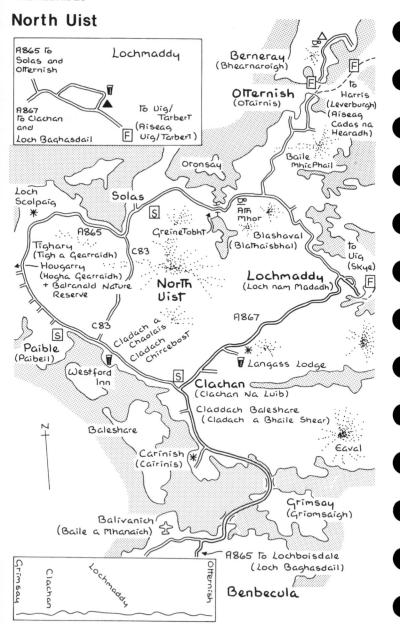

Lochmaddy

A865 To Solas and Otternish

A867 To Clachan and Loch Baghasdail

To Uig/Tarbert (Aiseag Uig/Tarbert)

Berneray (Bhearnaroigh)

Otternish (OTairnis)

To Harris (Leverburgh) (Aiseag Cadas na Hearadh)

Oronsay

Baile MhicPhail

Loch Scolpaig

Solas

S

GreineTobhT

ATh Mhor

Blashaval (Blathaisbhal)

A865

Tighary (Tigh a Gearraidh)

Hougarry (Hogha Gearraidh) + Balranald Nature Reserve

C83

North Uist

Lochmaddy (Loch nam Madadh)

To Uig (Skye)

F

A867

C83

Cladach a Chaolais Cladach Chircebost

Paible (Paibeil)

S

Westford Inn

Langass Lodge

S

Clachan (Clachan Na Luib)

Claddach Baleshare (Cladach a Bhaile Shear)

Baleshare

Carinish (Cairinis)

Eaval

Grimsay (Griomsaigh)

Balivanich (Baile a Mhanaich)

A865 To Lochboisdale (Loch Baghasdail)

Benbecula

Grimsay | Clachan | Lochmaddy | Otternish

NORTH UIST (UIBHIST A TUATH)

Grimsay – Lochmaddy – Otternish	**23.5 miles**
Grimsay – Tighary – Otternish	**30.5 miles**

From the road, North Uist is unremarkable. The A867 crosses open, peat-dug moorland; the A865 kisses the coast at Paible and Sollas, but much of the time runs across the machair with its grazing animals and deserted crofts, rather unromantic except in Spring. In truth the lattice of interlocking lochs and carved coast makes this a most dishevelled island.

Carinish (Cairinis) A religious site of medieval importance, though sadly decrepit. The Teampull na Trionard was founded by Beathog, the first Prioress of Iona.

Clachan (Clachan Na Luib) **S** The shop is the reputed birthplace of Bonnie Prince Charlie's faithful servant, Edward Burke.

Loch Scolpaid It is a Victorian folly, erected by Dr Alex MacLeod.

Sollas The eviction of crofters from Sollas by Lord MacDonald of Sleat in 1849, aided by policemen brought over from Skye, was one of the bloodiest in Scotland. 600 people, having already suffered extremes of hardship in the wake of the potato blight, offered a pathetic resistance (the 'battle of Solas'). Groups were dumped at various places of transit, and left, without food or shelter, to await the passage to Australia.

Lochmaddy (Loch Nam Madadh) **T S i** The main town of North Uist, with a museum and arts centre. The hotel once boasted 29 gillies to row the 29 boats on the 29 lochs managed by the hotel.

The Ferries Calmac operates a new (1996) vehicle ferry to Leverburgh (Harris) from Otternish (Aiseag Cadas na Hearadh) 3 or 4 times a day, connecting with the Berneray ferry (Aiseag Bhearnaraigh). The Uig (Skye) to Lochmaddy ferry sails once or twice a day.

The Islands Berneray (Bearnaraigh Na Hearadh) has around 150 inhabitants, a Gatliff hostel and a cafe. It is owned by Prince Charles. Boreray was occupied until recently, Pabbay was cleared for sheep last centry.

▲   Lochmaddy (01876) 500368
△   Gatliff, Isle of Berneray, 12 beds in a 'black house',
     GR 932814
🚲   (cycle hire) Morrison Cycle Hire, Bonnie View,
     19 Carinish, North Uist (01876) 580211

Atlantic waves on the shores of Harris: Photo. David Paterson

Harris

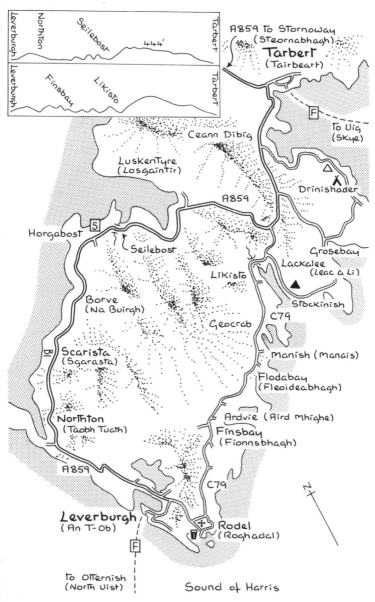

HARRIS (NA HEARADH)

Leverburgh – Finsbay – Tarbert	**23 miles**
Leverburgh – Scarista – Tarbert	**21 miles**

South Harris alone is worth the trip. The centre is mountain and rocky moor, and to reach Tarbert you have a choice. The contrast could not be greater. The A859 runs along the west coast, across the green machair, with the surf crashing onto huge white sandy beaches. Along the east coast runs the 'Golden Road', so called because of the building cost, which writhes like a snake through this barren, dramatic, impoverished land. During the Clearances the people were moved from the west coast to the east.

Harris continued to be the property of the MacLeods, living in Dunvegan (Skye), long after the MacKenzies had obtained Lewis. This only became a problem from 1706 when Norman MacLeod succeeded, as a baby, and inherited mountains of debt. He became known as the 'Red Man', and when he was old enough, added to the debt by embarking on a long career of drinking and gambling. When Johnson and Boswell visited Dunvegan in 1772 they described a lifestyle which their host, Norman MacLeod, grandson of the 'Red Man', could not afford. He turned to rack-renting, like the MacKenzie Lords of Lewis, displacing the tenants. Starving groups of islanders roamed the beaches, subsisting on raw shellfish and seaweed. Many died and many more emigrated. They were enticed by offers of a free passage and land in the New World, though, on arrival, often found themselves little better than slaves to a company, logging the virgin forest.

The end of the century saw Alexander MacLeod investing in Rodel, despite the frustrations of the salt tax, and the invasion of larger fishing vessels from the Clyde. As in Uist the Kelp industry grew, but the import of Spanish barilla in the 1820's halved the price of kelp. At the time the population of Harris was growing (under 2000 in 1755, 2,500 in 1792, 3,900 in 1831) and people were driven back to subsistence living on neglected land. The old communal run-rigs were broken up in favour of individual crofts. The island was sold, and in 1845 the potato blight struck. The Earls of Dunmore embarked on the standard practise of removing people who could not pay the rent, and leasing the land to sheep farmers. The displaced tenants were either given a free passage to Canada, or moved to the barren eastern seaboard. This had two consequences; the development of expert seamanship as most turned to the sea for a livlihood, and the growth of the tweed industry, which the Dunmore's helped to market.

The emigrees were settled mainly on Cape Breton Island, where each pioneer was adequately equipped. The enterprise was a model of its kind, and this helps to explain why Nova Scotia contains the one Gaelic-speaking community outside Scotland today.

By the early 20c Government intervention had stabilised life on the islands, and a wonderfully evocative account of growing up on Harris in the 1930's can be read in Finlay J. MacDonald's trilogy 'Crowdie and Cream', 'Crotal and White', and 'The Corncrake and the Lysander'.

Leverburgh (An T-Ob) 🍴 ☕ S The town into which Lord Leverhulme poured his last few years. It remains a workaday place, and the terminus for the ferry to Otternish (North Uist).

Rodel (Roghadal) 🍴 has an air of faded gentility and green luxuriance. The Church of St Clements was beautifully built about 1500 by the Eighth MacLeod of Dunvegan, with green sandstone shipped over from Mull. Rodel House was occupied by the MacLeods, the Earl of Dunmore and Lord Leverhulme. It became an hotel in 1923, and now stands empty and ghostly, though the bar remains welcoming. The village toilet provides impeccable welcoming relief.

Northton (Taobh Tuath) contains a ruined chapel and an important neolithic site.

Tarbert (Tairbeart) 🍴 ☕ S i Not touristy but full of tourists coming and going with the ferry to Uig (Skye), once a day.

▲ Stockinish (01859) 530373
△ Drinishader Hostel (01859) 511255
🚲 (cycle hire) Donald MacKenzie, Tarbert (01859) 502271
   Blazing Saddles, Tarbert

LORD LEVERHULME

Lord Leverhulme, the soap magnate, had never had a business failure when, as a 67-year old widower, in 1918 he purchased Lewis. Firstly he threw his energy into improving the fishing. The main problem was scarcity and glut, so he pioneered fish canning and dabbled with quick freezing. He reduced waste, putting dogfish into fishcakes, the offal to fishmeal and fertiliser, and the bones and heads into jelly and glue. In 'Macfisheries' he built up a chain of mainland retail outlets.

The other main business development was in weaving, as he introduced steel looms from Yorkshire in purpose built sheds at Ness, Barvas and Carloway. These have long since been dismantled, with weaving reverting to being a cottage industry, though most of todays tweed is produced in Stornoway mills.

By the end of 1919 he was building roads and constructing factories and houses in Stornoway, but there were objectors to his autocratic methods, and in particular to his wish to improve agriculture by destroying the crofting way of life. Eventually the Government sided with the crofters. Lord Leverhulme gave up; he donated land for 200 new crofts, then on his departure, made a free gift of the parish of Stornoway to its inhabitants, with all the houses and installations he had erected. Unemployment and destitution returned to Lewis after his departure, leading to the emigration of over 1000 able bodied men.

Leverhulme turned to Harris. He developed a port at Obbe, renaming it Leverburgh, and established a kippering industry. When he died in 1925, Leverburgh, which had cost £1/4 million to construct, was sold by the executors to a demolition company for £5,000.

In many ways Leverhulme was unlucky; many active men had been lost in the war; fishing was in decline; and Tuberculosis was rampant, the islanders having no ingrained resistance. Yet the wisdom of a complete outsider imposing his romantic notions, however benevolent, on whole communities, remains suspect.

Harris and Lewis

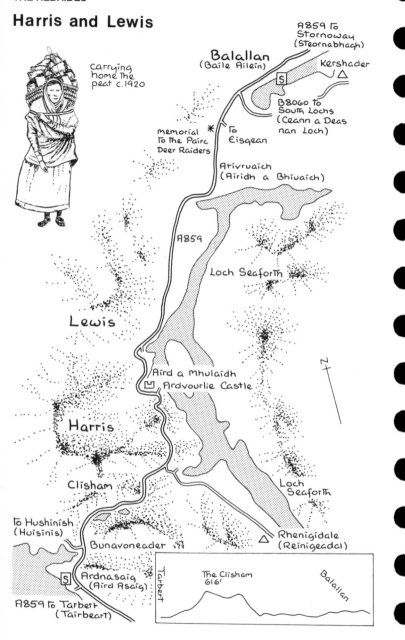

Carrying home the peat c.1920

A859 To Stornoway (Steornabhagh)

Balallan (Baile Ailein)

Kershader

S

B8060 To South Lochs (Ceann a Deas nan Loch)

memorial To The Pairc Deer Raiders

To Eisgean

Arivruaich (Airidh a Bhivaich)

A859

Loch Seaforth

Lewis

Aird a Mhulaidh

Ardvourlie Castle

Harris

N

Clisham

Loch Seaforth

To Hushinish (Huisinis)

Rhenigidale (Reinigeadal)

Bunavoneader

Ardnasaig (Aird Asaig)

S

Tarbert

The Clisham 616'

Balallan

A859 To Tarbert (Tairbeart)

HARRIS (NA HEARADH) and LEWIS (LEODHAS)

Tarbert – Balallan   20 miles

Harris and Lewis occupy the same island, the Long Isle, though such is the ruggedness of North Harris, that a hundred years ago travel between the two was mostly by boat. Nowadays the cyclist 'crosses the Clisham', a most dramatic road of soaring peaks, roaring burns and fabulous vistas. Keep an eye out for red deer, wild goats, blue hares, golden eagles and buzzards. It is a divide that is not merely physical, for there is rivalry between the people of Harris and Lewis, which can make for stimulating conversation. The crofting villages bustle with goats, chickens, sheep, enthusiastic children, and the shells of old lives, over-hung with the reek of burning peat. These provide welcome relief from the sections of E.C. funded 'superhighway', passing through acres of forestry, devastated in the mid-1990's by a plague of moths.

Bunavoneader An information centre is to be built above the remains of whaling piers, built by the Norwegians before the Great War, sold to Lord Leverhulme but closed in 1930. Further along the road Loch Chliostair feeds a hydro-electric power station which supplies most of Harris.
Beyond Hushinish is the island of Scarp, the scene of an experiment to sent post by rocket in 1938. Herr Zucker fired the rocket across the water, but, unfortunately, it exploded on impact.

△   Gatliff Rhenigidale (Reinigeadal), 11 beds, GR 229018
       Ravens Point Hostel, Co Chomunn na Pairc, Kershader,
       Lewis (01851)880236

THE HEBRIDES

Lewis (Balallan - Stornoway)

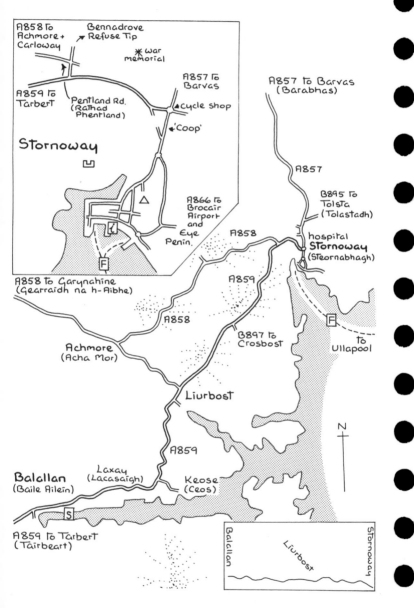

A858 To Achmore + Carloway

Bennadrove Refuse Tip

* war memorial

A857 To Barvas

A859 To Tarbert

Pentland Rd. (Rathad Phentland)

◄ Cycle shop

◄ 'Coop'

Stornoway

A866 To Brocair Airport and Eye Penin.

A858 To Garynahine (Gearraidh na h-Aibhe)

A857 To Barvas (Barabhas)

A857

B895 To Tolsta (Tolastadh)

hospital **Stornoway** (Steornabhagh)

A858

A859

F To Ullapool

B897 To Crosbost

Achmore (Acha Mor)

Liurbost

N

A859

Balallan (Baile Ailein)

Laxay (Lacasaigh)

Keose (Ceos)

S

A859 To Tarbert (Tairbeart)

Balallan | Liurbost | Stornoway

110

LEWIS (LEODHAS) BALALLAN – STORNOWAY

Balallan – Stornoway   **15 miles**

The MacKenzies established Stornoway as a fishing port soon after they became owners of Lewis in 1610. Although MacLeod is still the most common name, the MacKenzies took over the running of the island. It was, in the 18c, the usual tale of rack-renting and abuse of ownership, leading to evictions and emigration. The Chief also discovered an unusual way of making money from the islanders. In 1778 MacKenzie, Earl of Seaforth, offered to raise troops to fight in the American War of Independence, receiving a levy for each of the 1,082 men enlisted to the 78th regiment of Seaforth's Highlanders. These men were abused, maltreated and deprived of their pay. In Edinburgh they mutinied, before a settlement was finally reached, and they sailed for India!

The ownership of the MacKenzies ceased in 1843 when Lewis was sold to James Matheson, who had made a fortune in the China trade. He arrived on the eve of the potato blight, and helped alleviate its effects by importing meal and seed potatoes which he distributed, half as a gift, half as payment for public works. An efficient steamer service was established, and 17 schools endowed, English being the language of education, of course.

Matheson also employed Alexander Smith, one of the most respected agricultural improvers in Scotland. A very large part of the island lay under peat. When Matheson uncovered the stones at Callanish, they were buried to a depth of ten feet. Much of this peat lies on a layer of boulder clay, and where it had been cut for fuel, the soil was improved for crofters with shell sand and seaweed. Smith proposed that the peat moors be reclaimed, and that oil and tar be distilled from the peat. The latter venture was undercut by American oil, but the green pastures of Lewis show that, in places, reclamation has continued.

Before Matheson's death, his chamberlain on the island had provoked a riot on the island of Bernera with evictions, and after his death in 1882 his widow let the great sheep farm of Park to an English sporting industrialist. The natives took to raiding the sheep farm, and a detachment of the Royal Scots was sent in to quash the outbreak of lawlessness. Unfortunately, by 1900, landlessness was more acute on Lewis than elsewhere, for Matheson had avoided evictions by enabling such a large population to remain on the island. The stage was set for the philanthropist, Lord Leverhulme.

The road from Balallan to Stornoway is a long drag across inhospitable peat moor, accompanied by a roadside trail of Whyte and MacKay bottles and Irn Bru cans.

Keose (Ceos) The seaweed factory is a reminder of the short lived 18c kelp industry. It is now used as a food additive.

Stornoway (Steornabhagh) 🍴 ☕ Ⓢ ⓘ Rather old fashioned and bustling, but the urbanity of traffic fumes and disenchanted youth comes as a shock. It is the administrative centre of the Western Isles, and the main shopping centre. Fishing is still important; the oil industry is represented by the rig construction yard across the bay at Arnish Point; and the main ferry to Ullapool operates from here. Look for the Customs House (1830), the Western Isles Museum (Museum Nan Eilean), and Lewis Castle. This was the stronghold of the MacLeods of Lewis from the 13c, until it fell into the hands of the Seaforths. It is now a college.

The first battalion of the Seaforths was raised in 1777, and Lewis has provided fertile recruitment ever since. In 1919, 205 men returning from the war, drowned when their ship, HMS Iolaire, was wrecked outside the harbour.

△ Stornoway Hostel, 47 Keith St, Stornoway (01851) 703628
 Macrae Hostel, Torquil Terrace, Stornoway (01851) 703211
🚲 Alex Dan's Cycle Centre, 67 Kenneth St, Stornoway
 (01851) 704025
 Bikes of Stornoway, 1 Perceval Road North, Stornoway
 (01851) 702648

Stornoway, Lewis: Photo. David Paterson

Lewis (Callanish-Barvas)

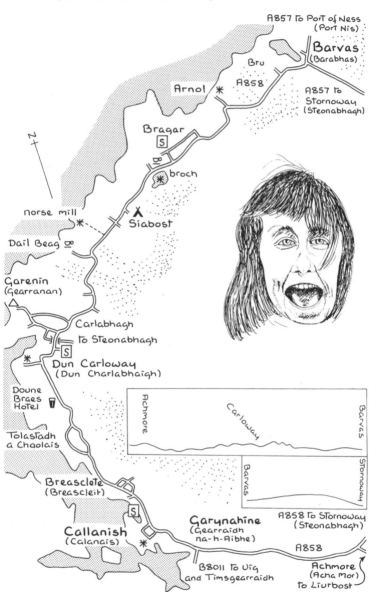

A857 To Port of Ness
(Port Nis)

Barvas
(Barabhas)

Bru

A858

Arnol ✳

A857 To
Stornoway
(Steonabhagh)

Bragar
[S]

broch ✳

norse mill ✳

Siabost

Dail Beag ∞

Garenin
(Gearranan)

Carlabhagh

To Steonabhagh

Dun Carloway
(Dun Charlabhaigh)
[S]

Doune
Braes
Hotel

Achmore | Carloway | Barvas

Barvas | Stornoway

Tolastadh
a Chaolais

Breasclete
(Breascleit)
[S]

Garynahine
(Gearraidh
na-h-Aibhe)

A858 To Stornoway
(Steonabhagh)

Callanish
(Calanais) ✳

A858

B8011 To Uig
and Timsgearraidh

Achmore
(Acha Mor)
To Liurbost

114

LEWIS (LEODHAS) CALLANISH – BARVAS

Liurbost – Callanish – Barvas   **27 miles**
Barvas – Stornoway   **12 miles**

The single-track A858 from Stornoway to Achmore (Acha Mor) takes some finding, as cars are encouraged to go via Leurbost (Liurbost). The middle of Lewis is, by and large, wild, windswept peat moor. The villages on the east coast are, in comparison, hives of humanity, both past and present. The A857 from Stornoway to Barvas (Barabhas) features the bog particulary well, with little else to distract the connoisseur.

Callanish (Calanais) 🍵 S The three megalithic stone circles were excavated from the peat in 1857. They comprise one of the most impressive archaeological spectacles in Britain. The new interpretive centre is low on interpretation but scores well for refreshments.
An old fish processing plant nearby is home to an innovative drugs company, employing 35 to transform fish oils into drugs for the treatment of life-threatening diseases.

Carloway (Dun Charlabhaigh) Amidst the crofting township, surrounded by the remains of blackhouses, a thirty feet high broch is one of the best preserved of these fortified dwellings. They date from the time when Scotland was slowly being converted to Christianity, though the dwellers must have felt more like snails. Broch's have been described as 'man's greatest architectural achievement in dry stone walling'.

Shawbost (Siabost) A tweed weaving centre, folk museum and renovated Norse Flour Mill.

Bragar Note the whale bone-arch, with the harpoon that killed it in 1921, hanging in the centre.

Arnol A blackhouse (Tigh Dubh) has been preserved as a museum.

△   Gatliff Garenin (Gearranan), 14 beds in a 'blackhouse',
       GR 193442 tel (01851) 643416

The megalithic stone circles at Callanish: Photo David Paterson

BONNIE PRINCE CHARLIE

On the morning of 22nd July 1745, Captain Durbé of 'Le du Teillay', a light frigate of 18 guns and a crew of 67, caught a glimpse of Berneray, the most southerly of the Outer Isles. Later that day 25 year old Prince Charles Edward Stuart, the 'Young Pretender', took his first look at the peat smoke drifting from the low, thatched 'blackhouses', the women working the patchwork run-rig arable fields, herd boys tending the sheep and black cattle, and the men with their primitive fishing vessels. He set foot on Eriskay, meeting Lord Boisdale, who tried to talk him out of the whole venture, then set off almost immediately for the mainland.

He landed at Loch nam Uamh (the Loch of the Cave), near Arisaig, and stayed a week at GlenBorrodale House, guarded by 100 men of young Angus MacDonald of Clanranald. The Highland chiefs were reluctant to join him, both MacDonald of Sleat and MacLeod of Dunvegan refusing, but the bandwagon began to roll, and on 31st October he marched south with 5000 men, having defeated Sir John Cope at Prestonpans. Carlisle fell and he reached Derby on 4th December, but the other elements of the plot, a general rising of Jacobites and Roman Catholics or a French invasion, failed to materialise and the retreat was begun. The retreat led, ingloriously, to Culloden, near Inverness, on 16th April 1746, where his men, half starved and exhausted, were routed with the loss of over 1000 dead.

Bonnie Prince Charlie spent the next six months running around the Highlands and Islands in a desperate game of hide and seek with the redcoats, with the price of £30,000 on his head (over £1 million equivalent today).

He returned to GlenBorrodale House via Loch Morar, four days after Culloden, and rowed out from there to Benbecula. Whilst on the islands 23 Royal Navy ships were engaged in the hunt.

Flora MacDonald was staying with her brother on South Uist when it was suggested that she escort the Prince to her home in Armadale (Skye). She met him on the night of 21 June, arranged for his disguise as Betty Burke, her Irish servant, and they left Rossinish in a four-oared ketch, hard gales helping them to elude the 270-ton naval sloop 'The Raven', though the crossing took 3 days and nights.

They landed near Uig in Loch Snizort, and whilst Charles was given provisions on the hill, Flora arranged for them to spend the night at Kingsburgh House. Here he allowed Flora to 'cut a lock frae his long yellow hair'. They parted at the 'Royal Hotel' in Portree, Charles skulking around Skye, then back via Mallaigvaig to GlenBorrodale House. He found it burned down with troops swarming everywhere, and took to the hills. He made his escape on 19th September leaving Loch nam Uamh, the same place he had set foot on the mainland for the French privateer 'L'Heureux'. He retreated to Europe to die of drink in 1788.

Flora MacDonald was taken prisoner soon after her parting with Charles, and put on board the 'Furnace', a notorious prison-ship under the sadistic Captain Ferguson. She spent the next 2 years in the Tower of London, but was then released and died in 1790 at the age of 68.

Following Culloden, the Highlands were devastated 'by fire and sword', and the Government followed this up with a series of Acts of Parliament designed to destroy those features of Highland life which made the Jacobite uprisings possible. Chiefs who supported the Jacobites were exiled and their estates forfeited to the crown; the Highlands were disarmed and local customs such as the wearing of the plaid and the playing of the bagpipes forbidden; and perhaps the most effective was the requirement of the chiefs to educate their sons and heirs at the English public schools. Within one or two generations the chiefs had been transformed into playboys and racketeering landlords. There are many reminders of this period. The failure of the Admiralty to catch the Prince resulted in the first systematic survey of the British coast, beginning with the Hebrides in 1748. The surveying was based on sightings of mountain cairns, and in this they were aided by army engineers, who were producing the first Ordnance Survey maps.

Sir Walter Scott's first novel, 'Waverley' was about the '45', written within living memory, and projected the Highlands in the public imagination as no previous book had done.

We sing the 'Banks of Loch Lomond' as a romantic ballad today, but it was written to commemorate the executions of the followers of Bonnie Prince Charlie. They were taken to London and there placed in the Tower of London, or in prison ships in the Thames. The 'high road' is death by gibbet, the 'low road' is death by drowning, and it was the souls of the executed men which journeyed north.

Skye

The hills of Ben Mor Coigach: Photo. David Paterson

Caledonian Canal and Ben Nevis: Photo. David Paterson

Overnight campsite above Uig, Skye: Photo. Tim Hughes

The Hills of Bla Bheinn from Loch Slapin: Photo. David Paterson

SKYE (AN T-EILEAN SGIATHEANACH)

Cycling on Skye. You don't have to cycle on Skye, yet the Mallaig – Armadale/Kyleakin – Kyle of Lochalsh section provides a useful link, as does the Uig ferry to North Uist or Harris. It is not, perhaps, the best island for the cyclist, too often plagued with bad weather, and quite touristy, a trend which the new Skye Bridge will encourage despite the cost. Included here are details of the main routes through, but, as the adjoining map indicates, there are other loops and spurs to quieter, more interesting, parts of the island.

Sixty miles long, yet so riven that no land is more than five miles from the sea, it was called Eilean Sgiatheanach, from the gaelic 'Sgiath', the 'Winged Isle'. To Ossian it was Eilean a Cheo, the 'Isle of Mist', and the Vikings named it Skuyo (pronounced 'Sky-a'), the 'Cloud Island'. It is high, hilly and wet, as the shopper said 'I think I need some more Tunes'. For all that much of it is grazed, and Skye is heavily crofted. Woodland can be found at the private estates of the Macleod and MacDonald chiefs, at Dunvegan and Armadale.

Visitors The mythical Celtic heroes were here. Cuchullainn, of the Ossianic poems, was the island chief. He went off to the Irish wars, leaving behind his fair wife, Bragela, and never returned to her. Fingal visitied the island, organising a great deer drive from Fingal's seat above Portree.
St Columba arrived here from Iona in 565AD, and doomed the paganism of the Celts.
Having fought, ravaged, plundered and killed in frequent raids, the Norsemen completed their domination of the islands by the 9c. For most of the next 500 years they ruled the Western Isles. Alexander the Third in 1263 challenged the Viking supremacy. King Haco mustered a fleet, sailing first to Lewis, then to Kyleakin to pick up reinforcements. A great battle was fought at Largs, and Haco, in defeat, escaped in his galleys, but was overwhelmed by a hurricane which wrecked much of his fleet off Lorne, Mull and Skye. He died at Kirkwall on the way home.
The Lords of the Isles, and their chieftains, held the island on behalf of the Scottish Kings, but, over the next two centuries

frequently rebelled against the throne, and undertook blood feuds among themselves. James the Fourth and, especially James the Fifth commanded submission. The latter mustered a great fleet which sailed from the Firth of Forth, reaching Loch Dunvegan via the Orkneys and Outer Isles. Here, Alexander, chief of the Clan MacLeod, was made prisoner, and the King sailed into Portree Bay, where, with much pomp and pageantry, he received the submission of the island chiefs.

Twenty eight years after the departure of Bonnie Prince Charlie, Dr Johnson and Boswell undertook their tour, and their writings did much to bring Skye to the attention of the broader public.

Ord, Skye: Photo David Paterson

Skye (Armadale - Broadford)

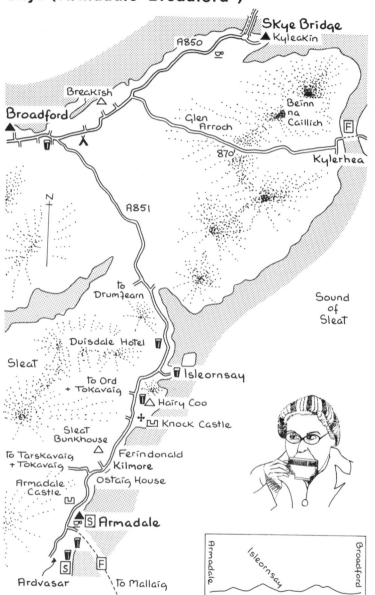

SKYE (ARMADALE – BROADFORD)

Armadale – Broadford   14 miles

The run from Armadale begins along a lush, lee shore, developing into boggy moorland towards Broadford. Beware of the 'ferry-rush'.

Armadale ☕ S 🍴 The neo-gothic castle was built in 1815 by Lord MacDonald of Sleat. It houses the Clan Donald Exhibition, and the stables, a cafe.

Knock Bay On a rocky mound is the ivy-clad stump of Camus Castle, a medieval stronghold of the MacDonalds. When Norway formally ceded the Isles to Scotland in 1266, Skye went to Angus the First, King of the Isles, who made a grant to Leod, son of a Norwegian prince. In the late 14c the Clan Donald took Sleat back from the MacLeods by force, and reoccupied Camus Castle.

When William of Orange sent two warships to the Sound of Sleat in 1690 to try to 'bring in' Sir Donald MacDonald, his clan fared better than their brothers in Glencoe. The naval raiding party had already burned down the chief's house in Armadale, when they were captured here at Knock, and strung up on gibbets made from their own oars on the beach by the castle.

Isle Ornsay 🍴 The lighthouse was built in 1857.
In the late 1870's the inhabitants were much terrified by the Beast of the Little Horn, though no beast was ever found.
On the other side of the Sound Gavin Maxwell wrote 'Ring of Bright Water'.

Broadford 🍴 S ☕ ⅈ The crofting centre of Skye. Broadford Hotel stands on the site of the inn at which Bonnie Prince Charlie shared his recipe for Drambuie. Beyond the village are the ruins of Coirechatachan, home of the chief of Clan MacKinnon, where Boswell and Johnson were entertained.

▲   Armadale (01471) 844260
       Broadford (01471) 822442
△   Bayview Bistro, Armadale, backpackers accomodation
       Ardvasar Bunkhouse
       Sleat Bunkhouse, Kilmore

THE HEBRIDES

Hairy Coo Backpackers Hotel, Teangue/Knock
Fossil Bothy, 13 Lower Breaknish, Broadford
(01471) 822297/822644
 (cycle hire) Ferry Filling Station, Ardvasar
(01471) 844249
Fairwinds Cycle Hire, and repair, Broadford
(01471) 822270

The hills of Knoydart from Isleornsay, Skye: Photo. David Paterson

Skye (Skye Bridge-Broadford-Sligachan)

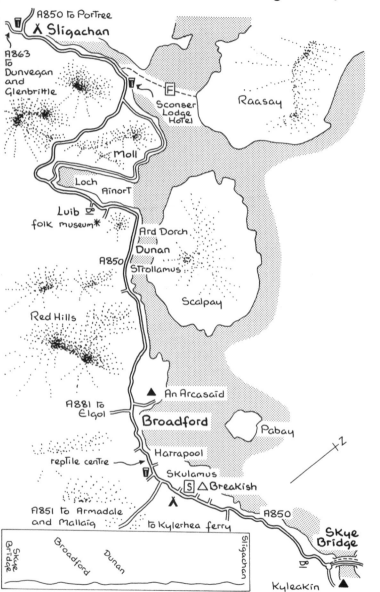

SKYE (SKYE BRIDGE – BROADFORD – SLIGACHAN)

Skye Bridge – Sligachan   25.5 miles

Cyclists cross the Skye Bridge for free, though it is a shame that the old A850 to Broadford has not been made into a cycle track. Traffic on the new road becomes a nuisance, though the one mountain 'pass' can easily be avoided by taking the old coastal road through Moll.

Sligachan is pivotal to the traveller on Skye. The inn is more of a roadhouse these days than a mountaineer's hole, though there is usually a scattering of small tents hereabouts. There follows a steady descent down Glen Varragill to Portree.

The mountains you see are really outlyers, the shapely Glamaig, Beinn Dearg, Marsco and Blaven (Bla Bheinn), but even these have a raw beauty and power, as muscular and well-thighed as a Greek God. The main Cuillin ridge is to the south, near Glenbrittle, though you can almost sense the brooding chasmic cauldron of these wonderful mountains.

Kyleakin (pronounced 'Kyle-Akin') 🍴 ☕ Ⓢ Once a charming fishing village protected by Castle Moil, ancient seat of the MacKinnons. The name derives from King Haco Hakonsson, King of Norway, who anchored his 160 ships here on the way to defeat at Largs in 1262.

Sconser At an inn here, in 1745, Clanranald, the envoy of Bonnie Prince Charlie, met the chiefs of the MacLeod and MacDonald clans, and learned that they had both decided not to throw in their lot with the Prince.

The Braes A battle here, in 1882, between crofters and Sheriff's Officers, backed by 47 Glasgow policemen, led to the setting up of a Royal Commission which produced legislation giving crofters security of tenure.

▲   Kyleakin (01599) 534585
Broadford (01471) 844260
Raasay (01478) 660240
Glenbrittle (01478) 640278
△   The Cliffe, Kyleakin (01599) 534778
Skye Backpackers, Kyleakin (01599) 534510

THE HEBRIDES

Fossil Bothy, 13 Lower Breaknish, Broadford
(01471) 822297/644

 Kyle Cycles, Kyle of Lochash (01599) 534842
Skye Bikes, The Pier, Kyleakin (01599) 534795
Fairwinds cycle hire and repair, Broadford (01471) 822270

The Red Cuillin Hills, Skye: Photo. David Paterson

Skye (Portree and Uig)

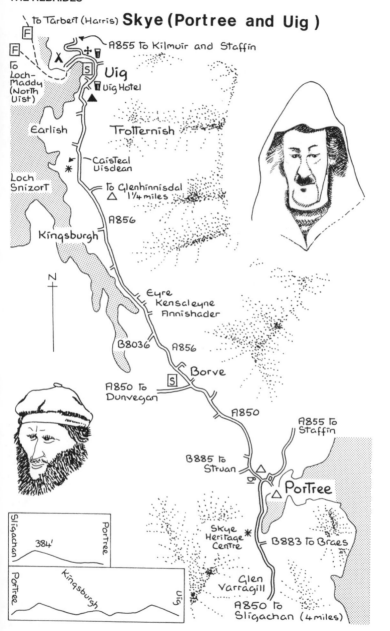

To Tarbert (Harris)

F

F

A855 To Kilmuir and Staffin

To Loch-Maddy (North Uist)

S Uig

Uig Hotel

Earlish

Trotternish

Caisteal Uisdean

To Glenhinnisdal △ 1¼ miles

A856

Loch Snizort

Kingsburgh

N

Eyre
Kensaleyne
Annishader

B8036   A856

S Borve

A850 To Dunvegan

A850

A855 To Staffin

B885 To Struan

Portree

Skye Heritage Centre

B883 To Braes

Glen Varragill

A850 To Sligachan (4 miles)

Sligachan   Portree

384'

Portree   Kingsburgh   Uig

SKYE (PORTREE AND UIG)

Sligachan – Uig   27 miles

Portree, the 'capital' of the island, is a pleasant, bustling place warranting a traffic warden. The direct route to Uig travels through a murky spaciousness, a worn and weathered landscape bristling with B & B's.

Portree 🍴 S ☕ i The name is derived from 'Port Righ' (King's Harbour) following the visit of King James the Fifth in 1540.

Trotternish The west coast of the peninsula has some of the finest farmland on Skye, but is mostly grassy moorland. Watch out for the golden plover, curlew, skylark, golden eagle and even the rare corncrake.

A twenty mile long ridge of Jurassic rocks runs down the spine of the peninsula. Most of the cliffs, including the Old Man of Storr and the Quiraing, are on the east side.

Kingsburgh The old house is where Bonnie Prince Charlie spent a night in 1746. Flora MacDonald and her husband later lived here, and entertained Dr Samuel Johnson in 1772.

Caisteal Uisdean (Hugh's Castle) The ruined 17c keep was built by a kinsman of the MacDonald chief. He was a bit of a pirate, and a rogue, and one day wrote, inviting the chief to a house-warming, intent upon murder. He also wrote to an accomplice giving details of the plan, and unfortuately for Hugh, this letter also reached the chief's hands. Hugh was put in a sealed-up dungeon at Duntulm with a lump of salt beef and an empty water jug.

Uig 🍴 S ☕ i The boat carrying Bonnie Prince Charlie and Flora MacDonald from North Uist landed just north of here at Skudaborg.

Today it has the small Isle of Skye Brewery, and the ferry terminal for Lochmaddy (North Uist) and Tarbert (Harris). There are one or two sailings a day, and none to Harris on a Sunday.

▲   Uig (01470) 542211
△   Portree Backpackers Hostel, Dunvegan Rd, Portree

THE HEBRIDES

(01478) 613641
Portree Independent Hostel, The Green, Portree
(01478) 613737
Glenhinnisdal Hostel
 Island Cycles, Portree (01478) 613121
(cycle hire) MacKenzies cycle hire, 5 Glenconnon, Uig

Loch Dhugaill and the Black Cuillin Hills, Skye: Photo. David Paterson

The North-West Highlands

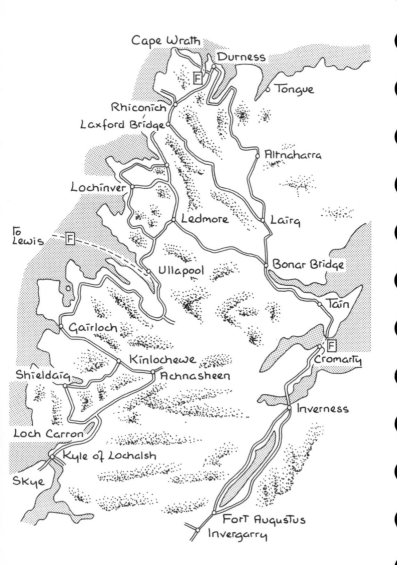

THE NORTH-WEST HIGHLANDS

From Kyle of Lochalsh the route north along the the coast takes you to the wildest, most rugged and most handsome corner of the British mainland. The north-south roads were made for tourists, and must be among the least travelled sections of tarmac in the country. The 'natural' routes lead east to the populated areas around the Cromarty and Moray Firths. Though only 50 or so miles apart the contrast between the two sides of Scotland is quite dramatic. For cyclists to the far north, the 'loop' has been completed using one of the three roads crossing the interior to Lairg and Bonar Bridge in the east, to connect with the railway.

A linking cycle route is included across the Black Isle to Inverness, and down through the Great Glen to Lochgarry and Fort William (see section 'Roads to the Isles'). The even more intrepid will continue across the top to John O' Groats. Details of the route south from there can be found in the companion volume to this book, 'Lands End to John O'Groats, the Great British Bike Adventure' by Phil Horsley.

Loch Carron

LOCH CARRON

Kyle of Lochalsh – Kishorn   **27 miles**

On single-track roads in the main, this run is all drama. The roads around Plockton could have been made for cyclists, beautifully wooded with glimpses of mountains and sea, spoiled only by such road signs as 'Sheep have no road sense – do Ewe'. The run around Loch Carron is rewarding, the views of the craggy ranges compensating for the steep pulls on the southern shore, and over to Kishorn.

Kyle of Lochalsh 🍴 ☕ S i The village developed with the coming of the railway. It is still the terminus for the line from Inverness, though the ferry to Skye was controversially replaced in 1996 by a toll bridge (cycles are free).

Plockton 🍴 S Its destiny as the beautiful, romantic summer haven you see today began when Hugh Innes bought the village in 1801. Innes had made his money as a sugar planter in the West Indies, and had no qualms about evicting his tenants for sheep, and planning a settlement of 280 houses. Only the lower part of the development was built. Across the bay is Duncraig Castle, built by Sir Alexander Matheson in 1841 on his return from the Far East, also with a fortune in his pocket, made by importing Indian opium into China. He resisted further clearances, but his successors carried on where Innes had left off. In 1946 the village was given to the National Trust for Scotland.
Craig Highland Farm, Plockton, is a rare breeds conservation centre.

Stromeferry (no ferry) In 1880 the S.S. Ferret, a vessel of 346 tons, was being used to tranship goods from the railhead at Stromeferry when it was stolen. Eighteen months later it was spotted by an eagle-eyed Glaswegian policeman, in Melbourne, Australia.
The medieval ruin of Strome Castle was once one of the principal west coast fortresses, and a stronghold of the MacDonalds of Glengarry. It was destroyed in 1602 during a long siege by English soldiers. The West Highland Dairy and Sheep Farm, Achmore is open to visitors.

Lochcarron 🍺 ☕ S i A lovely, long, straggling lochside village. There was once a good living to be made here, with hundreds of small boats shooting their nets in Loch Carron, but by the mid 19c the herring shoals no longer came into the sea-lochs and the runs of salmon and sea-trout dwindled. The village population was decimated, with people surviving on milk, potatoes, oatmeal and what fish they could catch, living in smoky cottages with wooden shutters in place of glass, and sharing the mud floor with their cattle. Visit the Smithy Heritage Centre.

Kishorn S ☕ (and Achintraid 🍺) An almost lush pocket of country, with a National Nature Reserve where natural trees and plants are allowed to regenerate, a rarity in Scotland. It became known in the mid 18c for the Kishorn dwarfs, two brothers and a sister, born to parents of normal stature, though the children were no more than 45 inches tall. Sadly they became travelling performers.

🚲 Kyle Cycles, Kyle of Lochalsh (01599) 534842

Liathach and Upper Loch Torridon: Photo. David Paterson

Glen Carron and Achnasheen

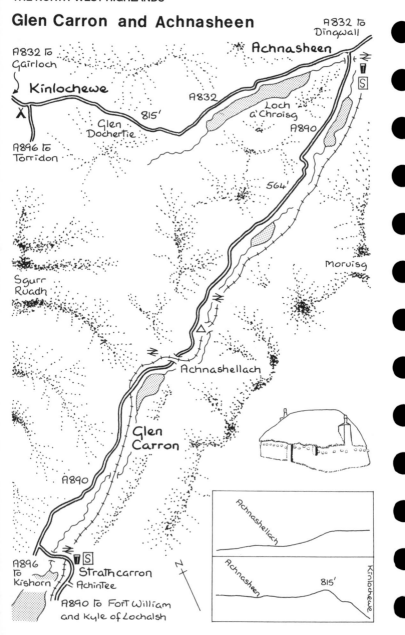

A832 to Dingwall

Achnasheen

A832 to Gairloch

Kinlochewe

A832

Loch a'Chroisg

A890

Glen Dochertie

815'

564'

A896 to Torridon

Morvisg

Sgurr Ruadh

Achnashellach

Glen Carron

A890

A896 to Kishorn

Strathcarron
Achintee

A890 to Fort William
and Kyle of Lochalsh

Achnashellach

Achnasheen

815'

Kinlochewe

142

GLEN CARRON and ACHNASHEEN

Strathcarron – Kinlochewe   **26.5 miles**

A steady run along the length of Glen Carron following the course of the railway, with passes over to Achnasheen, then back across to Kinlochewe. This is big, wide country, littered with monros and lesser peaks, home to soaring buzzards and very few people.

Glen Carron Although much of the valley sides has been taken by the Forestry Commission for conifers, the mile-wide strath is green and fertile. Along its 15-mile course to the sea the river Carron is swollen by innumerable torrents pouring off the mountains.

△   Gerry's Achnashellach Hostel, Craig, Strathcarron

Torridon

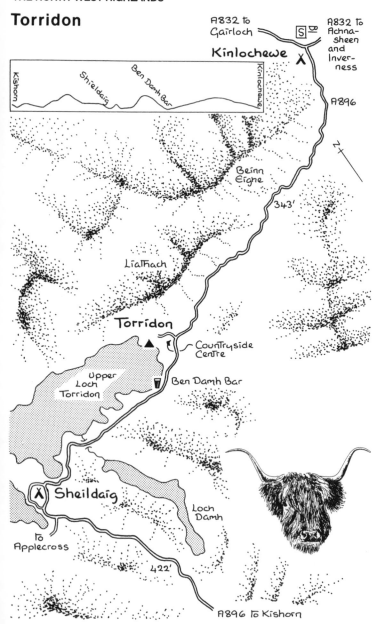

A832 to Gairloch

A832 To Achnasheen and Inverness

Kinlochewe

A896

Kishorn

Sheildaig

Ben Damh Bar

Kinlochewe

Beinn Eighe

343'

Liathach

Torridon

Countryside Centre

Upper Loch Torridon

Ben Damh Bar

Sheildaig

Loch Damh

To Applecross

422'

A896 To Kishorn

TORRIDON

Kishorn – Kinlochewe   **26 miles**

This run is dynamic; a tiny strip of single track road linking settlements clinging to the water's edge, amongst mountain scenery which can, correctly, be described a 'awesome'. The road is barely wide enough for a cycle and car to pass. You may meet coaches and caravans.

Applecross Turn left after Kishorn for the Bealach nam Bo (The Pass of the Cattle), a dramatic high pass cresting at 2054 ft. Applecross was one of the earliest seats of Christianity in Scotland, and well populated for a while. In 1792, 3000 black cattle were walked over the Pass on their way south to market, but the MacKenzies sold to the Duke of leeds, who sold to Lord Middleton in the 1860's, who cleared off the people and the cattle for the deer shooting. A new road now runs around the coast from Sheildaig.

Sheildaig 🍴 ☕ Ⓢ The name is from the Norse 'Sild-Vik' (Herring -Bay). The village was built around 1800 as a nursery for the Royal Navy, with grants for boatbuilding and fishermen. Unfortunately, by the time the new village was functioning and the men training to be 'mariners', Napoleon was history. The MacKenzies sold to the Duke of Leeds, who had the mariners 'cleared'. Its attractiveness attracts tourists, though the landscaping is not everyone's cup of tea.

After the Disruption of 1843 when the Free Church broke away from the Church of Scotland, and again, in the years after 1892 when the Free Presbyterian Church broke away from the Free Church, many services were held in the open whilst the Government church and manse were locked and empty. At the north end of Sheildaig a 2 metre high sheltering wall was built for the worshippers. At some point the minister's tent was replaced by a wooden pulpit (a similar survivor can be seen in the Gairloch Museum).

Torridon The Torridonian sandstones are amongst the oldest rocks in the world, laid down in shallow seas around 750 million years ago. In places they are capped with hard, white quartzite,

145

and some of the peaks gleam white. The ranges of Beinne Eighe and Liathach (the 'Grey One') are two of the finest in Scotland.

These lands were Mackenzie territory from the end of 16c to the 19c, although they were Stuart supporters and fought at Culloden. The lands were not taken from them after 1746 on the intervention of MacDonald of Sleat, who said 'Young Torridon is so popular with the ladies that if you hang him, half of them will hang themselves'.

In 1831 the glens were sold to Colonel McBarnet, a wealthy plantation owner from the West Indies who preferred sheep to tenants, and then to Duncan Darroch from Gourock, who wanted deer instead of sheep. He, however, saw no conflict with crofting and restored the lower grazing to crofters, and allowed some cattle to share the hills with the deer. When he died, at Torridon House, the tenants carried his body to Gourock for burial in the family vault.

The Coulin Forest, to the south-east of Glen Torridon is still a huge deer forest, and therefore closed to walkers from 20th August to 10th October. To the north-west is a 50 square mile nature reserve, aquired in 1951 and 1967, home to ptarmigan, wild cat, golden eagle, pine marten, peregrine, merlin, deer and wild goat. The great forest of native Scots Pine has largely vanished, but of great botanical interest is the high, natural alpine flora.

The Deer Museum and Countryside Centre is at Torridon.

▲   Torridon (01445) 791284
△   Inveralligin Field Centre (4 miles west of Torridon)
    (01445) 791247

LOCH MAREE

The name commemorates Saint Maelrubha, a missionary from Bangor in Ireland in the 7c. Off Talladale is the tiny Isle Maree, heavily wooded, on which the remnants of St Maelrubha's chapel can be seen. Two slabs mark the graves of a Norse prince and a daughter of a Celtic chief. A thousand years ago she began to doubt his love during the long periods he was away on expeditions, and pretended to be dead. He, in response, stabbed himself in the heart, and she, in remorse, plucked the dagger from his heart and plunged it into her own.

The isle was a pre-Christian sacred site, and pagan rites involving the sacrifice of a bull occurred here as late as the 17c. A well was a place of pilgrimage, its waters believed to have a powerful curative effect on lunatics, and a nearby tree was known for its spiritual properties. Queen Victioria made her offering in 1877.

Half way along the shore of the lake is Furnace. Though little remains now, 350 years ago it was the largest iron smelting plant in Scotland, built in the early 17c by Sir John Hay. The furnace denuded the surrounding hills of trees, though remnants of the old Caledonian Forest are being allowed to regenerate naturally hereabouts.

Loch Maree and Gairloch

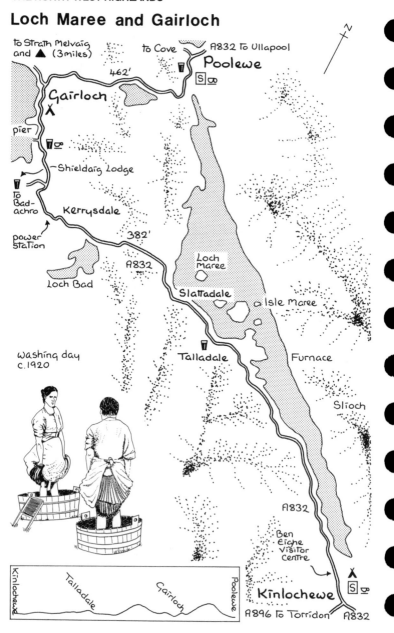

to Strath Melvaig
and ▲ (3 miles)

to Cove   A832 To Ullapool

Poolewe

462'

Gairloch

pier

Shieldaig Lodge

To Bad-achro

Kerrysdale

power station

382'

A832

Loch Bad

Loch Maree

Slattadale

Isle Maree

Talladale

Furnace

Slioch

A832

Ben Eighe Visitor Centre

Kinlochewe

A896 To Torridon   A832

Washing day c.1920

Kinlochewe   Talladale   Gairloch   Poolewe

148

LOCH MAREE and GAIRLOCH

Kinlochewe – Poolewe   23.5 miles

The A832 has been upgraded to two lanes, but, given reasonable weather, this whole section is not too fearsome for cyclists, with just one small climb over the Kerrysdale Pass. Loch Maree is, arguably, the finest fresh-water loch in Scotland, with Slioch (from 'Sleagh', a spear) outstanding. Behind this is a savagely complex mountain maze.

Kerrysdale Pass Formerly of exceptional beauty, but the rivercourse and waterfalls are often dry, the water being contained within the green pipe heading for the hydro-electric power station.

Gairloch ⚊ ☕ Ⓢ ⓘ The greater part of Gairloch was held by the MacLeods. Chiefly an island clan from Skye, Lewis and Harris, their mainland territories brought them into conflict with the MacKenzies, who held most of Ross. This culminated in a bloody incident in 1480, after which the King gave MacKenzie's brother a 'commission of fire and sword', and that was the end of the MacLeods of Gairloch.

The present village has a harbour, and is the centre of a whole group of crofting/holiday communities. Here, after the Great War, Lloyd George held an historic meeting with the Irish plenipotentiarities to discuss the Home Rule Settlement. Learn more in the Heritage Museum.

Loch Tollie The passage to Poolewe is over a barren moor. Loch Tollie has a crannog, used by Clan MacBeth as a refuge and stronghold.

▲   CarnDearg, Gairloch (01445) 712219
△   Achtercairn Hostel, Gairloch Sands (01445) 712131
       Badachro Bunkhouse, Badachro Inn (01445) 741255
🚲   (cycle hire) Glencairn Mountain Centre, Strath Square,
       Gairloch (01445) 712316

Loch Ewe and Little Loch Broom

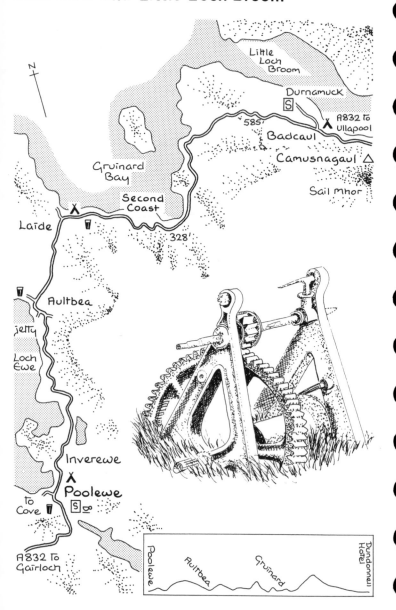

LOCH EWE and LITTLE LOCH BROOM

Poolewe – Dundonnell   **23.5 miles**

The corniche road twists along this torturous coast, with some leg-sapping pulls. The few crofts seem insignificant in this wild spaciousness.

Inverewe 🍵 In 1862 Osgood MacKenzie, the third son of the Laird of Gairloch, was given the barren, rocky peninsula by his mother. MacKenzie, one of a breed of adventurous, Scottish, plant collectors, created a sub-tropical garden out of nothing.

Loch Ewe In the last war, Loch Ewe was a naval base, the assembly point for Russian convoys. The base has since been developed by the Navy, giving the crofters of Aultbea some secure employment.

Laide 🍴 🍵 Ⓢ Here is a ruined chapel, said to be founded in the 7c by Saint Columba.

Second Coast At the waters edge is the ruin of an early 19c Watermill.

Gruinard is from the Norse 'Grunna Fjord' (shallow fjord), and is renown for its clean, sparkling, pink beaches. During the last war the Microbiological Research Establishment of the MOD used Gruinard Island for an experiment in germ warfare. Anthrax was disseminated in aerosol form to determine whether sheep could be affected. One result was the development of an effective vaccination for sheep, another that the island will be contaminated for at least 100 years.

△   Sail Mhor Croft Independent Hostel, Camusnagaul
     (01854) 633224
     The Bothy, Badrallach, Croft No.9, Dundonnell
     (01854) 633281

Dundonnell Forest and Loch Broom

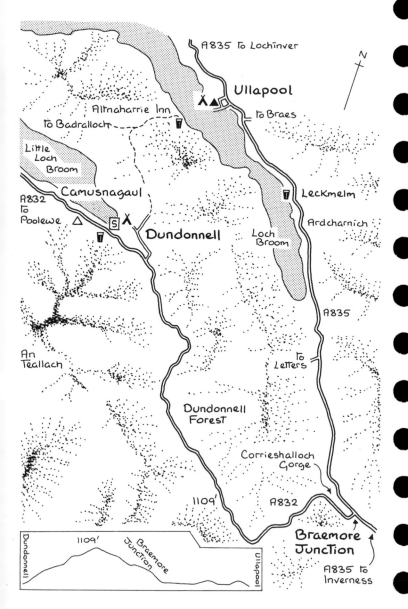

The Lonely roads of Lewis: Photo. Tim Hughes

Roisbheinn, Moidart: Photo. David Paterson

Liathach above Upper Loch Torridon: Photo. David Paterson

DUNDONNELL FOREST and LOCH BROOM

Dundonnell – Ullapool   **25 miles**

Prepare for this one. If your idea of fun is a thousand foot climb through desolate bleakness then this is for you. Of course, the descent is big too, and Strath More a proper fertile valley with gardens and trees.

An Teallach ('The Forge') is named for the smoke- like mists that curl around its eleven summits. This is golden eagle country, not for humans.

Dundonnell Forest Bleak moorland, this is a 'deer' forest. The road climbs to 1110 feet, and is a Destitution Road, made during the potato famine of 1851. To qualify for the meagre handouts of food, men had to put in a hard days labour on the roads. The women had to spin and knit. The very old, pregnant and crippled received special consideration, they only had to produce half the labour of the fit, but then they received half the ration too. Many of the small piers and roads up here were built like this.

Corrieshalloch Gorge Inland are the forests of Braemore and Fannich, covered during the Ice Age by an ice-cap several thousand feet thick, from which glaciers flowed to the Atlantic, melting and roaring down the Gorge at Corrieshalloch to Loch Broom. The Falls of Measach tumble in the Gorge.

Lael Forest Garden A Forestry Commission Arboretum.
Leckmelm Arboretum As at Lael, many of the trees and shrubs date from the 1870's.

Short Cut The possibility of a 'short cut' to Ullapool exists. Across Loch Broom from Ullapool is the Altnaharrie (Allt-na-h-Airbhe) Inn, renowned as one of Scotlands finest eating places (ie expensive). The ferry from Ullapool is privately owned and serves the Inn, but it has been known to take cyclists when they do not interfere with business. Phone in advance ((01854) 633230). The track across to Dundonnell is rough, and in places uncycleable.

153

Coigach and Ledmore Junction

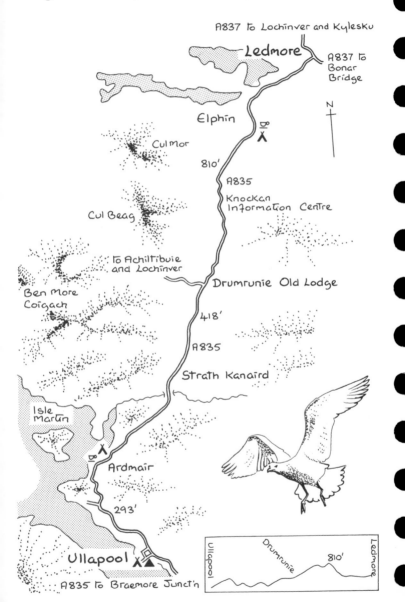

COIGACH and LEDMORE JUNCTION

Ullapool – Ledmore   17 miles

North of Ullapool is a glaciated plateau of gneiss, a myriad of little hills of great steepness with small glens and countless lochans, rich in birdlife. The Torridonian inland peaks are splendid, Stac Pollaidh, Cul Mor, Suilven and Quinag, as dramatic as any mountains in Scotland.

At Drumrunie Old Lodge there is a route choice. The direct route is along the A835 to Ledmore, then the A837 to Kylesku. Neither of them busy roads, this is an inland rollercoaster ride through this huge landscape. The alternative is to take the western boundary of the Inverpolly National Nature Reserve and follow the coastal road through Lochinver and Drumbeg, tiny roads with plenty of gear work, but a road made for cyclists, the coastal scenery as good as it gets anywhere. The A837 Lochinver to Skiag Bridge road offers an 'escape' route.

Ullapool 🍴 ☕ Ⓢ ⓘ Ullapool was a planned fishing village, founded in 1788. Loch Broom, in common with the whole of the west coast, teemed with prodigious shoals of herring. Fishing companies moved in, exporting the fish at vast profit. The boom lasted 50 years, and by 1880 the herring had been overfished out of existence. The trawlers now travel further afield, and, in winter, sell direct to Eastern European Klondyker factory ships, which spend the winter in Loch Broom procesing fish. So the town swaps its summer tourists for Romanians, Bulgarians and Russians, the crews changing every six weeks or so, the shops in Ullapool benefitting in the process. Visit the Ullapool Museum and Visitor Centre and the Loch Broom Museum. The main ferry link to the Western Isles sails from here to Stornoway.

Ardmair ☕ In the bay lies Isle Martin, with the ruins of an extensive fish-curing station.

Knockan The Visitor Centre is for the 27,000 acre Inverpolly National Nature Reserve.

Elphin ☕ The crofting community was established in 1812, one of the very few inland crofting townships in the northern

Highlands. The corrugated iron church was built in 1908 to a standard design for the United Free Church. The Highlands and Rare Breeds Farm is open to visitors.

▲   Ullapool (01854) 612254
    Ullapool Cycles, 11 Pulteney Street, Ullapool.

Little Loch Broom: Photo. David Paterson

Inverpolly

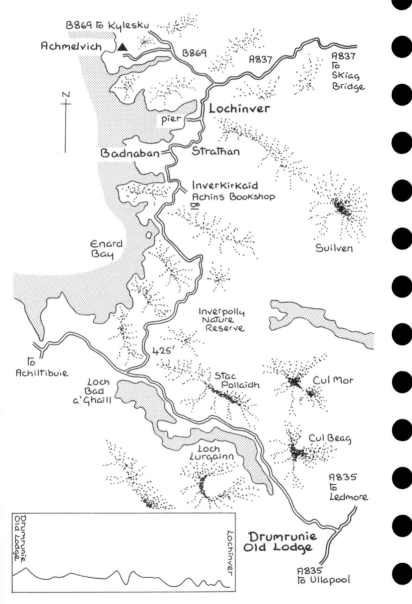

INVERPOLLY

Drumrunie Old Lodge – Lochinver   19 miles

An undulating, intimate section along tiny roads with birch-lined burns, exuberant birdsong, secret glens, rippling lochans and rock, bald wedges and slabs, the teeth of time. Magic.

Stac Polly (Stac Pollaidh), the 'stack of the bog'. The sandstone crest of this hill has lost its quartzite cap, and has been weather-shattered into pinacles.

Inverkirkaig A crofting township deriving its name from an 11c Culdee religious settlement run by an Abbot and 12 monks. They were allowed to marry, but their wives lived separately in Badnaban ('the village of the women or nuns'). Near the bookshop is a bridge marking the boundary of Assynt and between Wester Ross and Sutherland, the 'South Land' of the Vikings, coming here in 1034 and holding it until 1196.

Assynt The Clearances, begun in 1812, reorganised the parish into 5 large sheep farms. Over 160 families were evicted, mostly to coastal townships. The Sutherland estate came to exercise a tight control over people's lives, giving assistance as well as investing in sheep farming. From the 1880's, this was in severe depression, and much of the parish made over to deer forest. Assynt shared in the crofting unrest of the 1880's, and large areas were susequently handed over to the crofters as common grazing. Depopulation has continued, but in 1992 the purchase by crofters of the North Lochinver Estate was an historic achievement.

Lochinver A planned village, built by the Sutherland family in 1812 to house people cleared from the land, next to a successful herring smoking station at Culag. The Culag Hotel was, until 1888, a summer house for the Duke of Sutherland. The harbour has recently undergone a £6.5 million redevelopment.

From Lochinver the A837 is a relatively flat road to Skiag Bridge, whereas the coast road is totally stunning, twisting and turning like a snake, but also 'up and down like a bride's nightie'.

〶 (cycle hire) Assynt Mountain Bike Hire,

159

c/o Highland Stoneware, Baddidarroch, Lochinver
(01571) 844376

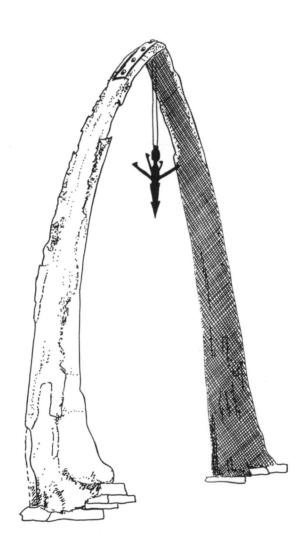

Badcall Bay, Scourie: Photo. David Paterson

Assynt

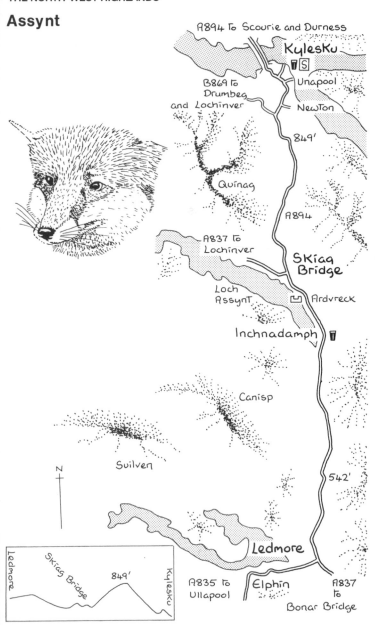

A894 To Scourie and Durness

Kylesku

Unapool

B869 To Drumbeg and Lochinver

Newton

849'

A894

Quinag

A837 To Lochinver

Skiag Bridge

Loch Assynt

Ardvreck

Inchnadamph

Canisp

N

Suilven

542'

Ledmore

Ledmore

Skiag Bridge

849'

Kylesku

A835 To Ullapool

Elphin

A837 To Bonar Bridge

ASSYNT

Ledmore – Kylesku   14 miles

The A837, the first road in Assynt, was begun at Inveran, near Bonar Bridge in 1821, and reached Lochinver a year later. A year after that a 'riding post' was initiated, then a mail-gig service carrying passengers as well as mail twice a week. In 1830 the road from Skiag Bridge to Kylesku and Durness was begun by the Duke of Sutherland.

In 1829 the chief of the Clan MacKay, Lord Reay, sold Assynt and the land to the north to George Leveson-Gower, who became the most hated man in the Highlands with the Sutherland clearances. Fifteen thousand men, women and children were evicted, driven to the sea and their homes burned, to make way for sheep. In recognition he was made Duke of Sutherland in 1833.

Suilven can be seen particularly well from Ledmore. Named by the Vikings 'the Sul-fjall' (the Pillar Mountain), its present name is from the gaelic 'Sul' and 'Bheinn'. It is capped with grey Quartzite scree.

Inchnadamph 🍴 ('the Stags Meadow)'. The hotel dates from at least 1736 and became, in 1830, a popular coaching inn. Limestone outcrops here, forming a green oasis. There are also limestone caves, in which, in 1926, were found the bones of artic animals, reindeer, cave bear, lynx and artic fox, and two human skeletons, the earliest known inhabitants of Scotland, 11,000 years old. Most of the people were 'cleared' from here in 1819.

Ardvreck Castle A private ruin, the clan centre for the MacLeods of Assynt.

Calda House Also a ruin. Built in 1726 for the Mackenzie laird of Ardvreck, it was burned down 11 years later in an ownership dispute.

Assynt and Stoer

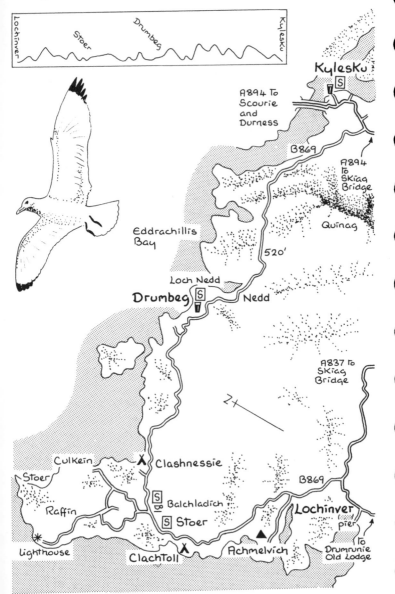

ASSYNT and STOER

Lochinver – Drumbeg – Kylesku   23 miles

The coast road from Lochinver to Kylesku is one of the most stunning cycle runs you will come across. It is not easy, with plenty of short, steep climbs, as steep as 25%, especially on the Drumbeg – Kylesku section.

The elegant tracery of the road kisses the coast, hugs cliffs, explores intimate glens and climbs crags of stone softened only by time and heather. Inland are indigo rocks, a thousand lochs and the magnificent Quinag; to sea the coast is a brilliant necklace with Eddrachillis Bay a string of pearls.

Achmelvich, Clachtoll, Clashnessie (☕ S), **Culkien and Drumbeg** (🍴 S) are small crofting communities with beautiful beaches.

Rhu Stoer Lighthouse Built in 1870 by two brothers of the famous Stevenson family, it was a family station until 1976, when it was automated and became a holiday home for lighthouse keepers.

Around the coast, a walk of a mile or so, is the Old Man of Stoer, a 200 foot sea stack. The coast hums with cormorants, fulmars, skuas, guillemots, gannets etc.

Kylesku (pronounced 'Kyles-ku') 🍴 S The ferry was established in 1830, (the Ferry Inn at the same time), replaced in 1984 by the award winning bridge. Boat trips will take you, via seal colonies, to Eas a Chual ('the Maidens Tresses'), at 658 feet the highest waterfall in Britain, at the head of the loch.

The ghost at the hotel is thought to be the brother of Miss MacKay, a famous landlady of the 1890's.

▲   Achmelvich (01571) 844480
△   Kylesku Lodges, Kylesku (01971) 502003

Scourie and Laxford Bridge

SCOURIE and LAXFORD BRIDGE

Kylesku – Rhiconich   **21 miles**

This road has recently been engineered into a two-lane highway for fish lorries which don't use it. For the cyclist, the difference between tackling this huge, wild, rough, lochan strewn moorland on narrow twisting, single track roads and a fast highway, however empty of traffic, is greater than would appear initially, but it's a lot better than cycling up the A1.

Reay Forest is the roughest, most intractable area of low country in the Highlands, loch-pocked, largely uninhabited, with just a few shooting lodges, the ancient hunting ground of the chief of the Clan MacKay.

Scourie 🍴 ☕ Ⓢ A crofting village cum holiday centre. In the bay, during the last war, the crews of British midget submarines trained for the successful attack on the German warship 'Tirpitz' in a Norwegian fjord.

Handa Island A dozen families lived here once, living off sea birds and their eggs. They were ruled by their own Queen and Parliament (the 'queen' being the eldest widow), but were forced to leave by the potato famine. Now uninhabited, it is an RSPB Reserve, good for spotting puffins, Artic and great skuas, eider ducks, razerbills etc.

Loch Laxford (from the Norse Lax-Fjord, salmon-fjord) is a deep, romantic fjord, fed by one of the finest salmon rivers in Scotland. On the north shore a boat shed contains the 'English Rose *111*', a 24 foot Yorkshire dory. She left Massachussetts on 4th June 1966, rowed by John Ridgway and Chay Blyth, landing on the Irish coast 92 days later. She is at John Ridgway's School of Adventure at Ardmore.

Rhiconich and Cape Wrath

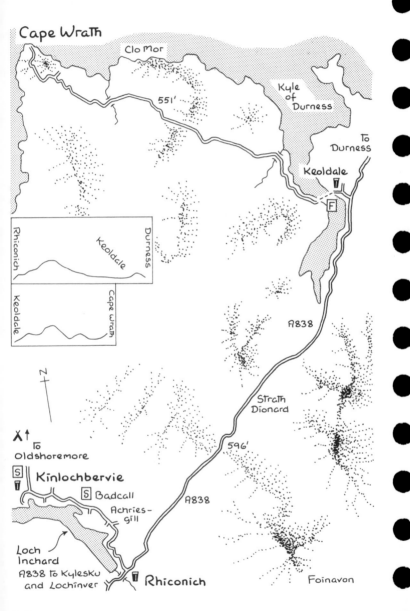

RHICONICH and CAPE WRATH

Rhiconich – Durness	**14 miles**
Keoldale – Cape Wrath	**12 miles**

Kinlochbervie 🍴 🅂 Not a twee village, but the third largest white fish port in Brtiain! The port, fish market and processing plant were developed in 1987/88, though improvements began 20 years earlier. Using mainly East Coast boats (stern trawlers and a few seine netters) and East Coast crews (transported in VW minibuses), the fishing is beyond the Outer Hebrides, a 2 or 3 day trip, returning with up to £25,000 worth , per boat, of whiting, squid, haddock, skate and monkfish, gutted and packed on board. How long before these fishing grounds also die in the face of such industrial fishing?

The Road to Durness Soon after Achriesgill the 'bumpiness' in the landscape caused by underlying gneiss is replaced with vast, even sweeps of hillside with grass replacing heather. At the watershed (594 feet) Gualin House was built as an hotel last century by the Duke of Sutherland.

Somehow this run is fitting for this wild corner of Britain. It is big country, wide open spaces, and improves in interest as the coast is reached. There are few signs of humanity, and the climb, though long, is not steep.

Cape Wrath From Keoldale (🍴) a small ferry crosses the Kyle of Durness, operating from May to September about 9 trips a day. The road then climbs over the dark, rolling moor of Parph to the most north-westerly point on the British mainland.

Parph is a gaelic rendering of the original Norse name for Cape Wrath, Hvarf, a 'Turning Point'. The lighthouse was built in 1827 by Robert Stevenson, and the roadway belongs to the Northern Lighthouse Commission. The sandstone moors thrust north at the Clo Mor cliffs, at 850 feet, the highest sea cliffs in mainland Britain. They are a huge sea-bird breeding ground, and, as recently as last century, swarmed with sea eagles. From Cape Wrath the islands are not usually visible, and due north there is no other land until you reach the North Pole.

Note that the road travels through a bombardment range, which can hinder progress.

Durness and Altnaharra

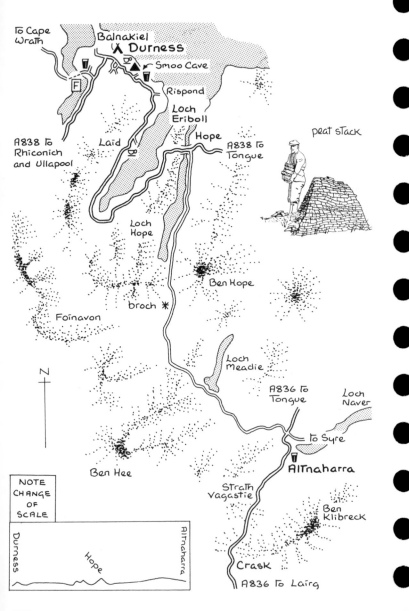

To Cape Wrath

Balnakiel

Durness

Smoo Cave

Rispond

Loch Eriboll

Hope

A838 To Tongue

peat stack

A838 To Rhiconich and Ullapool

Laid

Loch Hope

Ben Hope

broch ✳

Foinavon

Loch Meadie

A836 To Tongue

Loch Naver

To Syre

Altnaharra

N

Ben Hee

Strath Vagastie

Ben Klibreck

NOTE CHANGE OF SCALE

Durness

Hope

Altnaharra

Crask

A836 To Lairg

170

DURNESS and ALTNAHARRA

Durness – Altnaharra   37 miles

A long, relatively flat, ethereal run around the coast; followed by a wonderfully peaceful ride along the Strath, accompanying Loch Hope and birch woods, rimmed with mountains, particularly Ben Hope; then a steady climb over featureless moor, or rather a road featuring only moor.

Balnakiel ☕ An old radar station built to give us early warning of a nuclear attack, was abandoned in 1954, and converted into a craft village ten years later. Today it is a strange-looking cross-cultural place, with a mixture of the commonplace and inspirational.

Balnakiel means 'place of the church'. A Christian establishment was set up here in the 8c by Saint Maelrubha, though the present ruins date back to 1619. There is a monument to Robb Donn, the gaelic bard, and the south wall contains the 17c tomb of Donald MacLeod, a local thief and murderer.

Durness 🍴 S i is from the Norse Dyra-ness ('wolf Cape') for in Viking days wolves were the scourge of Cape Wrath.

The coast collapses into the sea in layers of cliffs and islands with white, sandy beaches and a blue/green sea. The clifftops contain many wartime relics.

The parish of Durness is fifty per cent larger than the old English county of Rutland, and the population density is one person per 96 acres.

Smoo Cave is a spectacular limestone cave, with boat trips to inner caverns.

Loch Eriboll was known in the last war as 'Loch 'Orrible' by thousands of servicemen based here. The island of Eilean Choraidh was used by the Dambuster Squadron to rehearse the attack on the 'Tirpitz', the scourge of the Russian convoys.

Dun Dornadilla Broch There is more to this than meets the eye.
Ben Hope At 3,040 feet, it is the most northerly munro.

▲   Durness (01971) 511244

171

LINK Section: Ledmore; Laxford Bridge; Altnaharra - Lairg

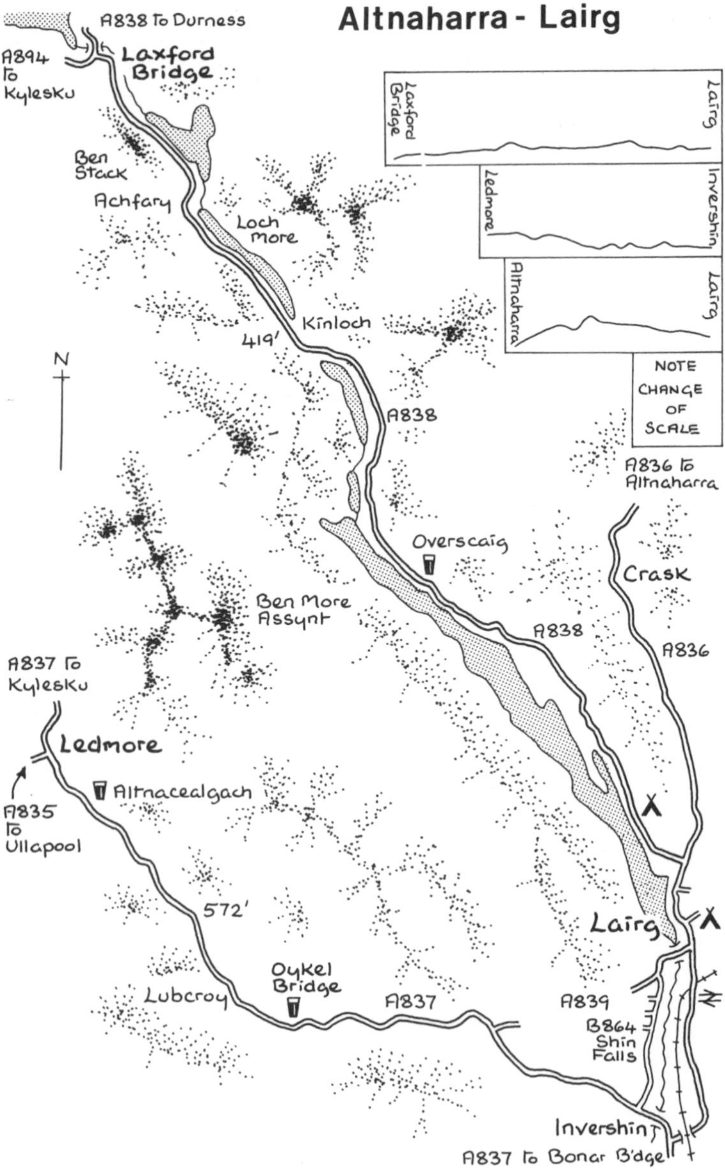

A838 To Durness

Laxford Bridge

A894 To Kylesku

Ben Stack

Achfary

Loch More

Kinloch

419'

A838

N

Overscaig

Crask

A836 To Altnaharra

Ben More Assynt

A838

A836

A837 To Kylesku

Ledmore

Altnacealgach

A835 To Ullapool

572'

Lairg

Lubcroy

Oykel Bridge

A837

A839

B864 Shin Falls

Invershin

A837 To Bonar B'dge

Laxford Bridge — Lairg

Ledmore — Invershin

Altnaharra — Lairg

NOTE CHANGE OF SCALE

LINK SECTION: LEDMORE/LAXFORD BRIDGE/ ALTNAHARRA – LAIRG

Ledmore – Bonar Bridge	**28 miles**
Laxford Bridge – Lairg	**34 miles**
Altnaharra – Lairg	**21 miles**

There are four routes which link the North West Highlands with Inverness. Most of the west coast settlements are isolated from each other, their lifelines running east to market. It is a suprise that, inland, the scenery cannot match the coast, but this is largely a matter of geology. The absence of a resident population of any size will, by now, come of no suprise to the cyclist in the Highlands.

Ullapool to Inverness (not marked on the map) The A835 through Garve to Strathpeffer and Inverness climbs over the Diridh Mor, or Great Ascent. At around 1000 feet, it is mainly dull and dreary moorland.

Ledmore to Bonar Bridge The single track A837 from Ledmore follows the famous salmon river, the Oykel.

Laxford Bridge to Lairg. The A838 from Laxford Bridge is single track, though mainly flat and straight. Be warned, this is the route used by the Kinlochbervie fish lorries, travelling fast at night in the main, yet it is the most attractive of the eastern routes, accompanied by lochs most of the way.

Altnaharra to Lairg The single track A836 from Altnaharra is, by and large, dreary.

Lairg ⊤ S ☕ i Gaelic for 'meeting place', the Lairg August sheep and lamb sale is the largest one-day market in Britain. Lairg is a pleasant, 'watery' town, the contents of Loch Shin powering a massive hydro-electric power station.

▲	Strathpeffer (01997) 421532
△	Aultguish Inn, by Garve (01997) 455254

LINK Section: Lairg - The Black Isle

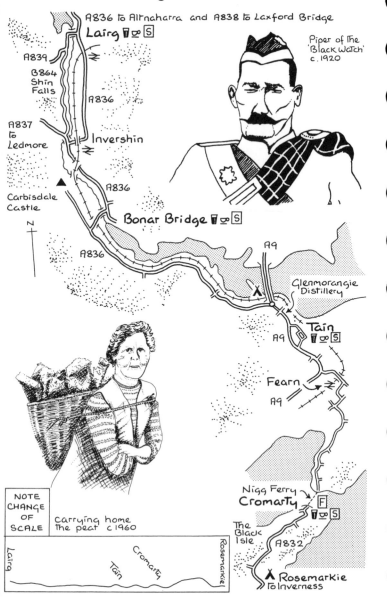

A836 to Altnaharra and A838 to Laxford Bridge

Lairg 🍺 ☕ S

A839

B864 Shin Falls

A836

A837 to Ledmore

Invershin

Carbisdale Castle

N

A836

Bonar Bridge 🍺 ☕ S

A836

A9

Glenmorangie Distillery

Tain 🍺 ☕ S

A9

Fearn

A9

Nigg Ferry
Cromarty F 🍺 ☕ S

The Black Isle A832

Rosemarkie
To Inverness

Piper of The 'Black Watch' c.1920

NOTE CHANGE OF SCALE

Carrying home The peat c 1960

Lairg — Tain — Cromarty — Rosemarkie

174

LINK SECTION: LAIRG – The BLACK ISLE

Lairg – Cromarty   **34 miles**

Lairg is a transitional town, beyond is definitely 'east', with a different feel to the landscape, different climate, different people. As a postscript to cycling the Western Highlands, a link route back to Invergarry is sketched over the next couple of pages. The route is as cycle-friendly as posible, and avoids heavy traffic where possible.

Tain 🍴 Ⓢ ☕ A smart, well heeled town, Scotland's oldest royal burgh with a Tolbooth, Mercat Cross, 'Tain through Time' Visitor Centre, and the Glenmorangie Distillery.

Nigg Ferry runs every half hour during the day from 1st April to 31st October.

Cromarty 🍴 Ⓢ ☕ Pleasant and friendly, the town has the Courthouse Museum and Hugh Millar's Cottage. Beauly, Cromarty and Dornoch Firths have resident populations of seals and otters. Dolphins and whales can be seen offshore.

Rosemarkie 🍴 Ⓢ ☕ 'The Riviera of the North' has an award-winning Pictish Interpretive Centre.

▲   Carbisdale Castle (01549) 421232
🚲   Tain Cycles (01862) 893332

LINK Section: The Black Isle - Inverness - Invergarry

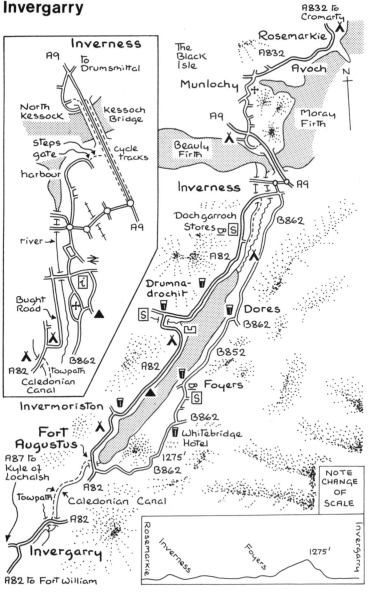

176

LINK SECTION: The BLACK ISLE – INVERNESS – INVERGARRY

Cromarty – Invergarry   57 miles

The recommended link route crosses the Black Isle to Inverness, then takes the B862 and B852 to the south of Loch Ness. The A82 is relatively flat, but busy with traffic.

Inverness 🍴 ☕ Ⓢ ⓘ The 'Capital of the Highlands' is a most pleasant small city, with lots of facilities, entertainment etc.

Drumnadrochit The Loch Ness Monster Exhibition Centre and Visitor Centre are on the west side of the loch. More than 1000 witnesses have testified to seeing the monster. The loch is the largest freshwater lake, by volume in mainland Britain.

Fort Augustus 🍴 ☕ Ⓢ ⓘ Previously called 'Kilcumain'. After the 1715 Jacobite rising, General Wade made this his HQ, and built the fort in 1729. 'Augustus' was William Augustus, Duke of Cumberland, at that time the fat, 8 year old son of King George the Second, later to become 'Butcher' Cumberland who defeated Bonnie Prince Charlie at Culloden, and thereafter allowed his troops to rape and pillage. The castle ruins became an abbey, then a private school, and home to 'The Young Clansman', a 'living' exhibition. The irony was lost on its creators.

▲   Inverness (01463) 231771
      Loch Ness (01320) 351274
△   Fort Augustus Backpackers Lodge (01320) 366233
      Foyers House Backpackers Bunkhouse, Foyers
      Loch Ness Backpackers Lodge, Coiltie Farmhouse,
      East Lewiston, Drumnadrochit (01456) 450807
      Inverness Student Hostel, 8 Culduthan Rd (01463) 236556
🚲   Bl Cycles, Inverness (01463) 715733
      Bikes of Inverness (01463) 225965
      The Cycle Works, Inverness (01463) 222522
      Wm Mitchell, Inverness (01463) 233478
      Thornton Cycles (01463) 222810
      (cycle hire) Wilderness Cycles, Drumnadrochit
      (01456) 450223

APPENDICES

Ferry Crossings
Caledonian MacBrayne Ltd (Calmac) are the major ferry operators. Brochures, timetables etc. are obtainable from head office:

Caledonian MacBrayne Ltd
The Ferry Terminal
Gourock
PA19 1QP
Tel (01475) 650100
Fax (01475) 637607
and from local offices.

Clyde Estuary
Gourock to Dunoon
Calmac Gourock tel (01475) 650100
Dunoon tel (01369) 706491

Gourock to Hunters Quay
Western Ferries
16 Woodside Gdns
Glasgow
G3 7UT
tel (0141) 332 9766

Arran
Ardrossan to Brodick
Calmac Ardrossan tel (01294) 463470
Brodick tel (01770) 302166

Lochranza to Claonaig (Kintyre)
Calmac

Islay
Kennacraig (Kintyre) to Port Ellen/Port Askaig (Islay)
Calmac Kennacraig tel (01880) 730253
Port Ellen tel (01496) 302209

Port Askaig to Oban via Colonsay
Calmac Oban tel (01631) 566688

Jura
Port Askaig (Islay) to Jura
Western Ferries

Mull
Oban to Craignure (Mull)
Calmac Oban tel (01631) 566688
Craignure tel (01680) 812343

Tobermory (Mull) to Kilchoan (Ardnamurchan)
Calmac Tobermory tel (01688) 302017

Barra and South Uist
Oban/Mallaig to Castlebay (Barra) and Lochboisdale (South Uist)
Calmac Oban tel (01631) 566688
Castlebay tel (01871) 810306
Lochboisdale tel (01878) 700288
Mallaig tel (01687) 462403

Eoligarry (Barra) to Ludag (South Uist)
MV Brendan (up to 12 passengers plus cycles)
Eriskay Enterprises Ltd
W Rusk tel (01878) 720233
J Campbell tel (01878) 720238

North Uist
Otternish (North Uist) to Leverburgh (Harris)
Lochmaddy (North Uist) to Uig (Skye)
Calmac Lochmaddy tel (01876) 500337
Uig tel (01470)542219

Harris
Uig (Skye) to Tarbert (Harris)
Calmac Uig tel (01470) 542219
Tarbert tel (01859) 502444

Lewis
Ullapool to Stornoway (Lewis)
Calmac Ullapool tel (01854) 612358
Stornoway tel (01851) 702361

Skye

Mallaig to Armadale (Skye)
Calmac Mallaig tel (01687) 462403
Armadale tel (01471) 844248

Glenelg to Kylerhea (Skye)
Roddy MacLeod tel (01599) 511302
This unique 'turntable' ferry operates from Easter to October.

Scottish Youth Hostel Association Hostels

	grade	telephone
Lochranza (Arran)	standard	(01770) 830631
Islay	standard	(01496) 850385
Inveraray	standard	(01499) 2454
Oban	superior	(01631) 562025
Tobermory (Mull)	simple	(01688) 302481
Glencoe	superior	(01855) 811219
Glen Nevis	superior	(01397) 702336
Armadale (Skye)	standard	(01471) 844260
Broadford (Skye)	superior	(01471) 822442
Kyleakin (Skye)	superior	(01599) 534585
Glenbrittle (Skye)	standard	(01478) 640278
Uig (Skye)	standard	(01470) 542211
Raasay (Raasay)	simple	(01478) 660240
Loch Lochy	standard	(01809) 501239
Ratagan	standard	(01599) 511243
Torridon	superior	(01445) 791284
Carn Dearg	standard	(01445) 712219
Ullapool	standard	(01854) 612254
Achininver	simple	(01854) 622254
Achmelvich	simple	(01571) 844480
Durness	simple	(01971) 511244
Tongue	standard	(01847) 611301
Carbisdale Castle	superior	(01549) 421232
Strathpeffer	standard	(01997) 421532
Inverness	superior	(01463) 231771
Loch Ness	standard	(01320) 351274
Howmore (S.Uist)	Gatliff Trust	–

Lochmaddy (N.Uist)	standard	(01876) 500368
Berneray (Berneray)	Gatliff Trust	–
Stockinish (Harris)	simple	(01859) 530373
Rhenigidale (Harris)	Gatliff Trust	–
Garenin (Lewis)	Gatliff Trust	–

Tourist Information Centres (telephone numbers)

Bowmore (Islay)	(01496) 810254
Broadford (Skye)	(01471) 822361
Brodick (Arran)	(01770) 302140/302401
Castlebay (Barra)	(01871) 810336
Craignure (Mull)	(01680) 812377
Dunoon	(01369) 703785
Durness	(01971) 511259
Fort Augustus	(01320) 366367
Fort William	(01397) 703781
Gairloch	(01445) 712130
Gourock	(01475) 639467
Inveraray	(01499) 302063
Inverness	(01463) 234353
Kilchoan (Ardnamurchan)	(01972) 510222
Kyle of Lochalsh	(01599) 534276
Lairg	(01549) 402160
Lochboisdale (S.Uist)	(01878) 700286
Lochcarron	(01520) 722357
Lochgilphead	(01546) 602344
Lochinver	(01571) 844330
Lochmaddy (N.Uist)	(01876) 500321
Lochranza (Arran)	(01770) 830320
Mallaig	(01687) 462170
Oban	(01631) 563122
Portree (Skye)	(01478) 612137
Shiel Bridge	(01599) 511264
Stornoway (Lewis)	(01851) 703088
Tarbert (Harris)	(01859) 502011
Tarbert (Argyll)	(01880) 820429
Tobermory (Mull)	(01688) 302182

Uig (Skye)   (01470) 542404
Ullapool   (01854) 612135

Useful Addresses

Scottish Tourist Board
23 Ravelston Terrace
Edinburgh
EH4 3EU
Tel (0131) 332 2433
Fax (0131) 343 1513

ScotRail
ScotRail House
58 Port Dundas Road
Glasgow
G4 0HG
Tel (0141) 332 9811
(0131) 556 2451
(01463) 238924

Cyclists Touring Club
69 Meadrow
Godalming
Surrey
GU7 3HS
Tel (01483) 417217

Sustrans Ltd
53 Cochrane Street
Glasgow
G1 1HL
Tel (0141) 552 8241

The Bike Bus
4 Barclay Terrace
Edinburgh
EH10 4HP
Tel (0131) 229 6274
(The Bike Bus operates regular runs for cyclists in Scotland)

British Cycling Federation
16 Upper Woburn Place
London
WC1H 0QE
Tel (0171) 387 9320

Rough Stuff Fellowship
4 Archray Avenue
Callander
Central
FK17 8JZ
Tel (01877) 30104

Scottish Youth Hostels Associtaion
National Office
7 Glebe Crescent
Stirling
FK8 2JA
Tel (01786) 451181
Fax (01786) 450198

The Association of Lightweight Campers
11 Grosvenor Place
London
SW1 0EY
Tel (0171) 828 1012